Massachusetts
— *in the* —
WOMAN SUFFRAGE MOVEMENT

Massachusetts
—— *in the* ——
WOMAN SUFFRAGE MOVEMENT

· ·

Revolutionary Reformers

Barbara F. Berenson

THE
History
PRESS

Published by The History Press
Charleston, SC
www.historypress.com

Front cover: Cover illustration by James Montgomery Flagg, October 28, 1915 issue of *Leslie's Illustrated Weekly*.
Back cover: Two suffragists distributing the *Woman's Journal* in 1913. A caption in a photo album compiled by Carrie Chapman Catt identifies them as Esther Abelson (*left*) and Mrs. J.L. Laidlaw (*right*); the Library of Congress identifies the woman on the right as Bostonian Margaret Foley. *Courtesy of the Library of Congress.*

First published 2018

Manufactured in the United States

ISBN 9781467118620

Library of Congress Control Number: 2017963226

Notice: The information in this book is true and complete to the best of our knowledge. It is offered without guarantee on the part of the author or The History Press. The author and The History Press disclaim all liability in connection with the use of this book.

To Rick, Daniel, and Alice

CONTENTS

ACKNOWLEDGEMENTS

I relied on many libraries, in particular the Schlesinger Library, Radcliffe Institute, at Harvard University. I also made extensive use of resources at the Boston Public Library, the Library of Congress, the Massachusetts Historical Society, the Minuteman Library System, and documents available in online libraries, especially Alexander Street's Women and Social Movements in the United States, 1600–2000, and Gale Primary Sources' Nineteenth Century Collections. I gained important insights by visiting Seneca Falls National Historical Park; the National Susan B. Anthony Museum & House in Rochester, New York; the Susan B. Anthony Birthplace Museum in Adams, Massachusetts; the Belmont-Paul Women's Equality National Monument in Washington, D.C.; and Marble House in Newport, Rhode Island.

I was fortunate to have excellent research assistance from several talented and delightful students: Elijah Berlin, Sarah Dahl, Evelyn O'Neil, and Julie Peng. Anita Danker of the Boston Women's Heritage Trail generously shared her research on Massachusetts members of the National Woman's Party, and Linda Stern and Helaine Davis graciously shared their research on local Jewish suffragists. I had an informative meeting with several members of the Worcester Women's History Project. Professor Peter Burgard of Harvard University provided important assistance.

Historians Susan Ware and Allison Lange, both experts on woman suffrage, offered many constructive comments on an early draft and throughout. Kasey Kaufman and Marya Van't Hul were wonderful brainstorming buddies. They also provided insightful comments on drafts, as did Josh Block and Melanie Goldstein. I also received helpful comments from Michael Baenen, Mona Hochberg, Joan Kenney, Marlene Rehkamp O'Brien, and Robin Tapper. Of course, all errors are mine alone.

It gives me great pleasure to thank Mary Ann Ashton, co-president of the League of Women Voters of Massachusetts, and Meryl Kessler, the executive director, for their enthusiasm. The League of Women Voters of the United States is the successor organization to the National American Woman Suffrage Association.

This is my second time publishing with The History Press. I am very pleased to have worked with editors Chad Rhoad and Abigail Fleming.

I owe special thanks to my sisters, parents, other family members, and friends. I am grateful for their patience and encouragement as I devoted so much of my time to this book.

I dedicate this book to my husband and children with love and gratitude. Rick was my daily sounding board, IT expert, and careful reader of my drafts. Daniel provided detailed comments on multiple drafts and helped me resolve how best to balance the national and state narratives. Alice and I have discussed woman suffrage since she wrote a high school paper about the post–Civil War schism in the movement. She also managed my collection of images and accompanied me to Seneca Falls and Rochester, New York. Their confidence in me made this book possible.

INTRODUCTION

As I wrote this book, I expected to witness the shattering of the nation's highest glass ceiling during the presidential election of 2016. That of course did not happen. Instead, the election proved a stunning setback for women seeking equal rights in American society. This modern-day result provides poignant insights into why it took eighty long years for the woman suffrage movement to succeed. Not only have a sizable proportion of men, then and now, disliked women gaining power, but women themselves do not constitute a monolithic bloc.

Women advocating for the right to vote faced difficulties that are almost unimaginable from our contemporary perspective. They had to challenge centuries of domestic tradition, church teachings, and legal doctrines that confined women to the domestic sphere and excluded them from civic participation. They lacked tools with which to seize or win power. Suffragists had to open women's eyes to their own lack of rights. They then had to persuade men, who possessed all the power, to share it. No wonder success required a campaign waged by three generations of courageous, visionary, and persistent women activists. Their victory was never inevitable.

This book tells the riveting story of woman suffrage with a focus on those women in Massachusetts who shaped both the national and state movements.[1] Why concentrate on this one state? Indeed, why emphasize the suffrage campaign in any state when women ultimately gained the vote through adoption of the Nineteenth Amendment to the U.S. Constitution? The answer is that the traditional story about woman suffrage, which focuses on the Seneca Falls Convention as the origin of the movement and Susan B. Anthony and Elizabeth Cady Stanton as the heads of it, omits essential parts of the full story.

The women's rights movement began in Massachusetts, the nation's most important abolitionist center. In 1837, Angelina and Sarah Grimké traveled throughout the state lecturing about the evils of slavery. When criticized for departing from a "woman's sphere," the Grimké sisters defended their right to have a voice in public debates about political issues. From the outset, they also set their sights on a larger prize. "I contend," Angelina Grimké wrote, "that woman has just as much right to sit in solemn counsel in Conventions, Conferences, Associations and General Assemblies, as man—just as much right...[to sit] in the Presidential chair of the United States."[2] She also presciently predicted the central role that Massachusetts would play in the movement. New England would, she wrote, "be the battleground, for she is most certainly the moral lighthouse of our nation."[3]

The Grimké sisters inspired a small band of bold women and men to defend a woman's right to publicly condemn slavery. Lucy Stone of Massachusetts took the next step in 1847. Committed to both women's rights and abolitionism, she delivered the first lectures devoted solely to what she described as the "elevation of her sex." The following year, several hundred women from upstate New York gathered at a convention in Seneca Falls, where Elizabeth Cady Stanton and Lucretia Mott led calls to end gender-based discrimination.

Stone and other Massachusetts-area activists decided the time was ripe to launch an organized, national women's rights movement. They hosted the First National Woman's Rights Convention in Worcester in 1850. Throughout the 1850s, these activists, soon joined by Susan B. Anthony, organized annual national conventions and worked to advance the rights of women while continuing to speak out against slavery. Though family responsibilities curtailed Stanton's travels, her incisive missives made her a key contributor.

When the Civil War began, activists placed the nascent women's movement on hold to concentrate on the crisis at hand. While many women assisted the Union army as nurses or assumed new roles on the homefront, Stone, Anthony, and Stanton joined the political effort to amend the Constitution to end slavery permanently. Once the bloody war ended and the Thirteenth Amendment was ratified, securing voting rights for the disenfranchised became the next battleground. The three expected their male associates from the abolitionist movement to seek expansion of the franchise to include women as well as black men. But their former allies prioritized black male suffrage. The Fourteenth Amendment, which introduced the word *male* into the Constitution, was adopted in 1868. The following year, Congress proposed the Fifteenth Amendment, which would grant the vote to black men but not to women.

In the wake of this exclusion, a schism divided the three women. Though disheartened, Stone supported ratification of the Fifteenth Amendment while pledging to continue the campaign for woman suffrage. Anthony and Stanton, however, opposed the Fifteenth Amendment because it omitted women. In 1869, the former friends, now bitter rivals, formed competing associations. Stone created the Boston-based American Woman Suffrage Association (AWSA), and Stanton and Anthony formed the New York–based National Woman Suffrage Association (NWSA).

Even after the Fifteenth Amendment was ratified in 1870, the schism continued. Stone found Anthony's and Stanton's racist commentary during the debate over the amendment unpardonable. The two camps sharply disagreed over strategy as well. NWSA concentrated on urging Congress to enfranchise women nationwide. AWSA recognized—correctly, as history would prove—that Congress would act only after suffragists had successfully persuaded a critical number of individual states to grant women the vote. AWSA supported the growth of state and local suffrage associations and worked with them to wage a series of state campaigns. Stone also founded the Boston-based weekly newspaper the *Woman's Journal*, which was the communications hub of the woman suffrage movement.

Why is the work of AWSA, arguably the more vital branch of the divided suffrage movement, not better known? During the acrimonious schism, Anthony and Stanton molded historic memory by writing an influential one-sided account of the first decades of the movement. Their version elevated their own importance and that of Seneca Falls and minimized (and in some instances, virtually erased) the essential contributions of Lucy Stone, the Worcester Convention, and AWSA. The dominance of their account continues today. The proposed redesign of the ten-dollar bill, for example, features Anthony and Stanton but not Stone. One goal of this book is to raise Lucy Stone and her local allies to their rightful stature in the suffrage narrative.

Near the end of the nineteenth century, a younger generation of suffragists, including Lucy Stone's daughter, Alice Stone Blackwell, persuaded the aging rivals to reunite and form the National American Woman Suffrage Association (NAWSA) in 1890. Though NAWSA was not headquartered in Massachusetts, it was the strategic successor to AWSA—except, unfortunately, in the area of race relations. NAWSA strengthened state suffrage associations and intensified support for state suffrage campaigns. After her mother's death in 1893, Stone Blackwell became editor of the *Woman's Journal*, which remained the organ of the suffrage movement until women were enfranchised.

Another goal of this book is to explore the hard-fought state suffrage campaigns waged in Massachusetts. These battles offer a window into the particular challenges the suffrage movement faced in northeastern, urban, industrialized states. Moreover, the repercussions from these campaigns shaped the strategies of the national movement.

When Lucy Stone formed AWSA, she anticipated that Massachusetts would promptly grant women the vote. Despite its reputation in modern times as a liberal and progressive state, however, Massachusetts led the deep and prolonged resistance to woman suffrage. Privileged women who favored the status quo organized in opposition to their own right to vote. Many men believed women voters would reject or at least neglect their domestic responsibilities. Men who opposed Prohibition worried that women voters would back restrictions on the sale of alcohol. Republican Yankee elites feared women would support the labor movement, while Democratic Irish Catholics feared the suffrage movement's association with an ugly nativist strain in the Republican Party. The nineteenth century ended with the stinging defeat of an advisory referendum that set back the entire suffrage effort.

Election Day! By E.W. Gustin. This anti-suffrage cartoon illustrates the fear of many men at the prospect of women's rights. *Courtesy of the Library of Congress.*

At the dawn of the twentieth century, Maud Wood Park and other intrepid suffragists, many of them young and college-educated, revived the movement. They formed new alliances and piloted new techniques, many of which influenced the movement far beyond the state's borders. Eventually, their efforts convinced the Massachusetts legislature to submit a proposed state constitutional amendment to enfranchise women to the voters in November 1915. Suffragists ran a zealous and inventive campaign. But the state continued to be a center of anti-suffrage activism, and a sizable majority of the all-male electorate rejected the amendment. The male voters in New York, New Jersey, and Pennsylvania rejected similar amendments that same year.

Defeat again led to a major transformation within the suffrage movement. NAWSA decided the time had come to pursue a federal amendment. This strategic shift took advantage of the substantial clout of women voters in the West, where eleven states had enfranchised women. It also responded to the rise of Alice Paul's militant National Woman's Party, which focused entirely on a federal amendment. Maud Wood Park moved to Washington to lead NAWSA's lobbying efforts in Congress.

The climax of the long campaign for suffrage unfolded against the backdrop of World War I, which, as suffragists reminded politicians and the public, the United States had entered to "make the world safe for democracy." In 1918, when the U.S. Senate failed to pass a suffrage amendment by one vote (the House had passed the amendment), Massachusetts suffragists once again sprang into action. Relying on techniques honed during past campaigns, they led a successful effort to replace a U.S. senator opposed to suffrage with a supporter. This victory in formerly recalcitrant Massachusetts made clear to fence-sitters which way the wind was blowing. The Senate voted for the Nineteenth Amendment. Following ratification by Massachusetts and thirty-five other states, it became part of the U.S. Constitution on August 26, 1920.

Note: To guide the reader through the intersecting national and Massachusetts stories, I emphasize principal organizations, main events, and key leaders. Although a diverse group of women and men contributed to the movement's eventual success, most of its leading figures were native-born, educated, white Protestant women, and they receive the bulk of my attention. I do consider, however, the important contributions of several Catholic, Jewish, and African American suffragists and show how nativism, classism, and especially racism tainted the suffrage movement. In the end, the Nineteenth Amendment was a great but imperfect victory. Much work remained—and remains—for future generations.

1
The Birth of a Movement

The whole land seems roused to discussion on the province of woman, & I am glad of it." Angelina Grimké penned these words on July 25, 1837, in the small North Shore town of New Rowley, Massachusetts, one of many stops on her statewide antislavery lecture tour.[1] During that summer, the state's residents participated in a public debate unlike any ever seen before. On one side were Angelina Grimké, her sister Sarah, and a small group of abolitionists who publicly supported the Grimkés' right to address "promiscuous" (mixed-gender) audiences to advocate for an immediate end to slavery, itself a highly divisive subject. On the other side was the formidable authority of both church and custom, which held that only men, the undisputed heads of the family unit, should inhabit the public sphere of politics and commerce. Women, in contrast, should be restricted to the domestic sphere of child-rearing, housekeeping, and moral and religious education. In the face of this powerful "separate spheres" ideology, the Grimké sisters refused to retreat. Instead, they challenged the traditions that made women silent and subordinate. Their remarkable Massachusetts tour would move women in front of the podium and launch the nation's women's rights movement.[2]

The Grimké sisters were the daughters of a wealthy slaveholder in Charleston, South Carolina. The events that led them to abandon their privileged lives and become radical reformers began in 1819, when Sarah, then twenty-seven years old, accompanied her ill father to Philadelphia so he could consult with Quaker physicians. Sarah was drawn to the Quaker community and their beliefs, which condemned slavery. When she returned to the South, she shared her reflections with Angelina, her younger sister by twelve years. After their father's death, the sisters, by then firmly opposed to slavery, moved to Philadelphia and became Quakers.

The Grimkés' early years in their new home coincided with a northern religious revival movement known as the (Second) Great Awakening. Religious reformers preached that salvation required working toward the moral perfection of individuals and society. The Awakening spawned a wide range of social-reform movements, including the abolitionist and temperance movements. Women, who played the primary roles in their families' moral and religious lives, also began to venture outward. "As women, as wives, as mothers, we are deeply responsible for the influence we have on the human race," wrote Maria Weston Chapman, who would organize the Grimkés' Massachusetts speaking tour.[3]

The Grimkés became linked to Massachusetts through abolitionist William Lloyd Garrison. In 1831, he chose Boston as the home for the *Liberator*, the nation's first newspaper dedicated to the immediate end of slavery. He and a small band of allies also trained antislavery "agents" to lecture at any gathering that would have them. In that era, public lectures were a major source of both education and entertainment. In 1833, Garrison and his allies formed the American Anti-Slavery Society to support and publicize the efforts of the local antislavery societies sprouting in the New England and mid-Atlantic states. Lucretia Mott, a Quaker who had spent most of her childhood in Nantucket, Massachusetts, organized the Philadelphia Female Anti-Slavery Society. Angelina Grimké attended Mott's meetings and voraciously read the *Liberator*.

When Garrison launched his antislavery crusade, few white northerners cared to question the South's "peculiar institution." The North's thriving textile, transportation, and banking industries depended on the southern plantation economy. As the abolitionist movement grew, some northern men disrupted antislavery meetings and threatened Garrison. He reported these events in the *Liberator*.

Angelina Grimké wrote to Garrison to express her support for his goals and her dismay at the mobs that sought to silence him. "It is my deep, solemn, deliberate conviction that [abolitionism] is a cause worth dying for," she stated.[4] He immediately recognized the significance of her letter. He and other northern abolitionists lacked personal exposure to slavery's horrors. Angelina's letter promised a southern witness who could provide firsthand accounts.

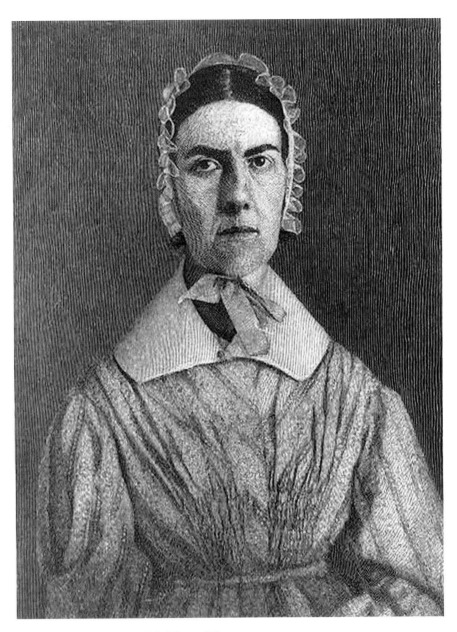

Angelina Grimké. *Courtesy of the Library of Congress.*

Garrison invited the Grimkés to become the first women antislavery lecturers. Even though he and his colleagues anticipated that the sisters would speak only to women, this was nonetheless a radical proposition. Only men lectured publicly on political issues. Even those women who had ventured into the antislavery world had confined their appeals to small groups of female friends and neighbors rather than delivering lectures to large audiences of strangers.[5] The Grimkés accepted Garrison's unusual invitation. They trained in New York City and, by January 1837, had addressed attentive audiences of women in that city.

The American Anti-Slavery Society planned to hold its annual meeting in New York City in May 1837. Women were invited—but only as spectators. Maria Weston Chapman, a Garrison ally and leader of the racially integrated Boston Female Anti-Slavery Society, saw an opportunity. She proposed holding the first-ever convention of antislavery women at the same time. She hoped to stimulate the formation of additional female antislavery societies and increase the number of women willing to circulate antislavery petitions that would be submitted to Congress. Petitioning was the one political act allowed women of that era.

Chapman's idea proved spectacularly successful. Two hundred women from nine northern states, including the Grimké sisters and Lucretia Mott, convened for this extraordinary gathering. Nearly twenty black women attended, with Maria Stewart, formerly of Massachusetts, among them. She had been the original woman trailblazer in antislavery public speaking, though her efforts had not led to a sustained movement. Her short-lived foray into the public realm had begun in 1831, when she delivered several lectures in Boston in which she denounced racism and slavery and exhorted women to become moral leaders of the black community. When she addressed audiences that included men as well as women, detractors criticized her public role. Angry and frustrated, Stewart left Boston in 1833. Her attendance at the 1837 women's antislavery convention marked a rare return to the world of public affairs.

Maria Weston Chapman. *Courtesy of Boston Public Library*.

Convention delegates in New York endorsed a series of resolutions, including one declaring it the duty of every woman, northern or southern, to petition Congress to end the interstate slave trade. At Angelina's urging, the delegates took a further step, one reaching beyond abolitionism to directly challenge the confines of the woman's sphere. "The time has come," she announced, for woman to "no longer remain satisfied in the circumscribed limits with which corrupt custom and a perverted application of Scripture has encircled her." A woman's duty, she continued, is to use "her voice, and her pen, and her purse" to help overthrow American slavery. The convention proceedings record that this resolution prompted "an animated and interesting debate respecting the rights and duties of women." Angelina's resolution was adopted, though not unanimously.[6]

On the heels of the convention, the Grimké sisters received their next assignment from the American Anti-Slavery Society: to lecture throughout Massachusetts to persuade women to sign antislavery petitions and to form and join antislavery societies.

THE GRIMKÉS' SPEAKING TOUR

Angelina and Sarah arrived in Boston in late May 1837. Angelina wrote to Jane Smith, her best friend from Philadelphia, that in view of the prevailing public attitude toward women, she and Sarah were walking on an "untrodden path." "I feel as if it is not the cause of the slave only which we plead, but the cause of woman as a responsible moral being," Angelina declared. She also noted her delight in finding "a very general sentiment" prevailing among Boston's women abolitionists "that it was time our [women's] fetters were broken."[7]

Before the Grimké sisters began their lecture tour, Maria Weston Chapman wrote to female antislavery societies throughout the state urging them to assist the sisters' efforts. Women, she said, must refute the idea that their moral and spiritual obligations were unequal to those of men.[8] Although Angelina and Sarah traveled together, Angelina, the more confident public speaker, delivered nearly all of the addresses.

Some men, as well as women, attended Angelina's lectures, particularly as reports of her eloquence circulated. In North Weymouth, for example, the audience of about 120 included 30 men. In Lynn, a crowd of nearly 1,000, including many men, packed into the Methodist church. She was delighted, writing to Jane Smith, "It is wonderful to us how the way has been opened for us to address mixed audiences, for most sects here are greatly opposed to public speaking for women." Angelina credited "curiosity in many and real interest in the [antislavery] cause in others" with prompting attendance.[9]

Opponents sought to silence the Grimkés, however. The leaders of the influential Congregational Church prepared a letter that they ordered ministers to read from every pulpit. It warned that the "appropriate duties and influence of women…are unobtrusive and private." Serving as a public reformer, the ministers claimed, would cause a woman's character to become "unnatural" and pave the way for "degeneracy and ruin."[10] Lydia Maria Child, another of Garrison's associates, mocked the ministers' letter. "Women have changed the household utensil into a living, energetic being," she wrote, "and [church leaders] have no spell to turn it into a broom again."[11]

But the belief that women had no business entering the public sphere had widespread support and many influential spokespersons, including Catharine Beecher, the elder sister of Harriet Beecher Stowe, who would later write *Uncle Tom's Cabin*. At first glance, Catharine Beecher seems an unlikely choice to defend the traditional woman's role. An educator from a reformist family, she had established the Female Seminary in Hartford, Connecticut, to provide the daughters of the middle and upper classes with a rigorous education.

Beecher believed, however, that the purpose of a woman's education was to prepare her to best fulfill her subordinate roles as wife and mother. Beecher was confident that the more educated a woman becomes, "the more she can appreciate the wisdom of that [divine] ordinance that appointed her to her subordinate station."[12] She published a critique of the Grimkés' views. The arguments Beecher articulated concerning how women should use their increased opportunities for education would divide women into pro- and anti-rights movement camps for decades. Her attitude also demonstrates the impossibility of predicting the factors that would lead any particular woman to embrace or rebel against convention.

Defying their critics, the Grimkés persisted. By the end of the summer, Angelina had delivered over eighty lectures and addressed over forty thousand people. The sisters had collected thousands of signatures on antislavery petitions. They next turned their formidable skills and energy toward refuting the claims of the Congregational ministers and Catharine Beecher.

Sarah Grimké. *Courtesy of the Library of Congress.*

At the request of Mary Parker, the president of the Boston Female Anti-Slavery Society, Sarah wrote a series of public letters (addressed to Parker) on the "province of women." Her far-reaching letters shattered every argument offered to defend the subjugation of women. She placed the blame for women's inferior status on church leaders, whom she accused of misreading scripture, and on ordinary men, whom she accused of treating women as either household drudges or "dressed-up toys." She also criticized the laws that perpetuated this state of affairs. "There are few things which present greater obstacles to the improvement and elevation of woman to her appropriate sphere of usefulness and duty," Sarah wrote, "than the laws [that] destroy her independence and crush her individuality…[laws which] she has had no voice in establishing."[13]

Angelina wrote public letters to Catharine Beecher. These letters primarily focused on abolitionism, as Beecher also opposed immediate emancipation.

But Angelina reiterated her belief in the moral equality of the sexes, stating that the ideology of separate spheres robbed women of their natural right to think, speak, and act. She succinctly explained her philosophy: "[W]hatever it is morally right for man to do, it is morally right for woman to do. Our duties are governed, not by difference of sex, but by the variety of gifts and talents committed to our care."[14]

The Grimkés expected scathing criticism from opponents. They were discouraged, however, when some of their own abolitionist allies criticized the sisters' outspokenness on women's rights. Some abolitionists believed that women belonged in the domestic sphere. Others, while sympathetic to women's desire to actively support the abolitionist movement, argued that the subject of women's rights was a distraction from the antislavery struggle. Theodore Weld, who had trained the Grimké sisters as lecturers and would soon propose marriage to Angelina, was among the latter. As southerners, he told them, "you can do ten times as much on the subject of slavery" as northern-born women. He urged them to let their antislavery advocacy refute those who claimed that women should not speak in public. "Let us first wake up the nation to lift millions of slaves of both sexes from the dust," he continued, "and it will [then] be an easy matter to take millions of females from their knees and set them on their feet."[15]

The sisters disagreed. Angelina reminded him that it was the ministers' letter that "roused the whole country to inquire what right we had to open our mouths." She explained that rights must be asserted when they are denied. She added that women must establish the right to speak publicly in order to "do any good in the anti-slavery cause."[16]

By the end of the epochal summer, Angelina and Sarah were exhausted and ill with typhoid fever and bronchitis, respectively. Angelina never fully recovered her strength; in less than a year, both sisters would largely retire from public life. But first, Angelina broke an additional barrier; she became the first woman in the United States to address a legislative body.

Many Massachusetts lawmakers, even some not sympathetic to the antislavery movement, were appalled when the pro-slavery forces that dominated the U.S. Congress enacted gag rules to prevent the body from considering antislavery petitions. In response to this assault on free speech, the Bay State legislature appointed a special committee to consider antislavery petitions. The committee chair, abolitionist Henry B. Stanton (who would later marry Elizabeth Cady), permitted Angelina to present petitions signed by twenty thousand Massachusetts women.

On two days in February 1838, Angelina spoke at the Massachusetts State House before an overflow crowd of five hundred. The audience included supporters, detractors, and the merely curious. She told the assembly that she owed it to both the suffering slave and the deluded master to campaign to overthrow slavery. To those who opposed her role in the public sphere, she announced, "American women must care about this subject" not only because it is moral and religious but also "because it is political."[17]

Several months later, Theodore Weld and Angelina Grimké married in Philadelphia as abolitionists gathered for both the annual meeting of the American Anti-Slavery Society and the second annual convention of antislavery women. Angelina and Weld modified the traditional wedding vows. She did not promise to "obey," and he rejected the authority of laws that gave him control over his wife's property.

The following day, on May 16, 1838, the convention of antislavery women met in Pennsylvania Hall, a new building largely financed by abolitionists. But as the convention began, a disruptive crowd hostile to the abolitionist movement gathered outside. Delivering what would be her last public address for thirteen years, Angelina told the audience that it was the protestors who "should fear and tremble. The current is even now setting

Fire destroys Pennsylvania Hall. *Courtesy of the Library of Congress.*

fast against them."[18] The following night, a mob burned Pennsylvania Hall to the ground.

The next month, the married couple and Sarah—who would continue to live with her sister—moved to New Jersey. The trio scoured southern newspapers for articles, letters, and ads depicting the cruelties of slavery. These formed the basis of *American Slavery as It Is: Testimony of a Thousand Witnesses*, published in 1839. Angelina had three children and, with her husband and sister, founded a small, progressive boarding school to educate the children of abolitionists.

Many in the antislavery movement wondered what had led the Grimkés to abruptly withdraw from public life. Both were exhausted, but they also had another point to make. Some of their critics had alleged that their "unnatural" actions had rendered them unsuitable for family life. "It is absolutely necessary that we should show that we are not ruined as domestic characters," explained Angelina. "I verily believe that we are thus doing as much for the cause of woman as we did by public speaking."[19]

By the end of 1830s, the Grimké sisters' lecture tour had launched the women's rights movement. Their retirement message had anticipated one of the movement's unending battles. Their efforts also inspired other activists to take the next step on the long road to equal rights. Lucy Stone of Massachusetts and her allies would do so when they expanded the reach of the fledgling women's movement beyond the confines of the abolitionist campaign.

2

THE CONVENTION DECADE

Lucy Stone never forgot when, as a nineteen-year-old farm girl attending church in the central Massachusetts town of West Brookfield, she heard her minister read the 1837 letter condemning the Grimkés for their departure from a "woman's sphere." She made her cousin, who was sitting beside her, "black and blue with the indignant nudges of my elbow at each aggravating sentence."[1] A decade later, Stone would become the first female college graduate in Massachusetts and invent a new occupation: lecturer for women's rights. She would work to expand rights for women until her death in 1893.

Stone grew up familiar with the burdens of women. A perhaps apocryphal story reports her mother's greeting to her newborn daughter: "Oh dear! I am so sorry it is a girl. A woman's life is so hard." Stone realized this truth at a young age. She resented that her father was often a harsh master of his wife and children and that her brothers received a superior education. Still, this was a household steeped in abolitionist ideas, and her father subscribed to Garrison's *Liberator*. Allowed to speak her mind on this topic, Stone became committed to abolitionism. A fearless child with a strong temper, she grew into a young woman determined to continue her education and avoid marriage.

Stone became a primary school teacher in 1834, at age sixteen. For the literate, native-born, white women who would populate the ranks of the early suffrage movement, teaching in rural schools or the few female academies was virtually the only alternative to a life of unrelenting domesticity. Stone's way to additional education was stymied at first. Her father applied most of her earnings to retiring his farm debts and financing her brothers' education. After five years of teaching, she had managed to save enough money to enroll in the recently opened Mount Holyoke Female Seminary. But when a sister died, Stone left school to help care for her nieces and nephews. She was bristling with resentment of a woman's plight when she attended a local lecture by abolitionist activist Abby Kelley. Like Stone, Kelley was from Worcester County and had been a schoolteacher before the Grimkés inspired her to become an antislavery lecturer. Kelley's foray into the public sphere would in turn inspire Stone.

When Stone learned that Oberlin College in Ohio was coeducational (it also admitted black students), she decided to save enough money to study there. In 1843, at age twenty-five, she enrolled. Yet she discovered gender inequities existed even at the liberal college. She was paid less than male students who performed the same housekeeping and tutoring chores. In addition, the school restricted its female students from speaking in public. A superb student, Stone was invited to write an essay for her 1847 commencement. She declined when she learned that, unlike male students, she would not be permitted to deliver her own remarks.

While at Oberlin, she had opportunities to hear visiting abolitionists deliver lectures. After attending one of Abby Kelley Foster's (Kelley married abolitionist Stephen Foster in 1845), Stone wrote her an enthusiastic note: "[M]y heart dances gaily at the remembrance [of your remarks]."[2] In reply, Kelley Foster urged Stone to become an antislavery lecturer in Massachusetts after her graduation.

Stone agreed to the suggestion, but she also had larger aims in mind. She wrote her mother that she intended to address both slavery and "the elevation of my sex." She sent her sister, who claimed she "knew of no respect in which women were oppressed," a pamphlet containing a sermon Unitarian minister Samuel May had delivered in Syracuse, New York, in May 1845.[3] In *Rights and Conditions of Women*, he argued, "Women are coaxed, flattered, courted, but they are not respected by many men as they ought to be; neither do they respect themselves as they should." Women should have the opportunity to contribute to the "commonweal," he asserted. May advanced the radical proposition that the "disenfranchisement of females is as unjust as the disenfranchisement of males would be" because nothing in women's "moral, mental, or physical nature disqualifies them to understand correctly the true interests of the community, or to act wisely in reference to them."[4] Stone agreed.

Left: Lucy Stone as a young woman. *Right*: Abby Kelley Foster. *Courtesy of the Library of Congress*.

In 1847, she delivered her first speech in support of women's rights in the Gardner, Massachusetts, church where her brother Bo served as minister. She argued that education would "ennoble" women's lives and permit "grand and glorious uses."[5] Stone then moved to Boston to become a paid lecturer for the Massachusetts Anti-Slavery Society. For six dollars a week, she maintained an arduous travel and speaking schedule. She was widely praised as a persuasive and engaging speaker with a melodious voice. But she also faced considerable hostility. Before an antislavery lecture in Malden, a pastor—who had been asked to give notice of her talk—announced that "a hen will undertake to crow like a cock at the Town Hall this afternoon."[6]

Although hired to protest slavery, Stone made sure to also criticize women's lack of rights. When some abolitionists complained about the dual focus of her lectures, she declared, "I was a woman before I was an abolitionist."[7] She subsequently renegotiated her agreement with the Anti-Slavery Society: she would lecture on women's rights on weekdays and slavery on weekends. Her decision to deliver some lectures solely on women's rights began a new era in the nascent women's rights movement.

As Stone rode the lecture circuit in Massachusetts, activists in upstate New York held two local women's rights conventions. These conventions marked the first occasions women came together in convocations called for the express purpose of discussing their rights. The first one is the best remembered.

THE SENECA FALLS CONVENTION

The idea for a women's rights convention originated when Lucretia Mott visited her sister in Seneca Falls, New York, during the summer of 1848. Mott rekindled her friendship with Elizabeth Cady Stanton, whom she had met eight years earlier. Stanton, the daughter of a successful lawyer in Johnstown, New York, was born in 1815 and educated at the Troy Female Seminary (later renamed in honor of its founder, Emma Willard). Some of Stanton's formative memories were of gender inequity. She was heartbroken when her father greeted her repeated academic successes by openly wishing that she were a son. Reading her father's law books, she discovered at an early age that laws protected the rights of men but not women.

She met her future husband, abolitionist attorney Henry Stanton, at the home of her cousin Gerrit Smith. After their wedding in 1840, Henry brought his wife to meet the Grimké sisters. The couple then traveled to London, where Henry served as a delegate to the World Anti-Slavery Convention. In the spectators' gallery, Elizabeth Cady Stanton met Lucretia Mott, who had been denied a seat with the male delegates. Stanton wrote the Grimké sisters, "I have had much conversation with Lucretia Mott & I think her a peerless woman."[8]

The couple lived in Boston until 1847. During those years, Stanton bore three children; she would later have four more. The family then moved to Seneca Falls, where Henry hoped to start a political career. The Finger Lakes region had become a hub of reform during the Great Awakening, and the Erie Canal had made it a bustling economic center.

After moving to upstate New York, Stanton longed for engagement beyond her domestic duties. When Mott visited in July 1848, the two women reconnected. Over afternoon tea, Stanton shared her dissatisfaction with a woman's lot in life. The five women present, who also included Martha Coffin Wright (Mott's sister), Mary Ann M'Clintock, and Jane Hunt, decided to act. They issued a call to the first-ever Women's Rights Convention, where

Left: Elizabeth Cady Stanton with daughter Harriot in 1856. *Right*: Lucretia Mott later in life. *Courtesy of the Library of Congress.*

attendees would discuss "the social, civil, and religious condition and rights of [American] women." [9]

Several factors likely precipitated this extraordinary decision. All of the women except Stanton, a non-Quaker, were members of the Progressive Friends, a newly formed radical Quaker faction that gave women an equal voice in religious meetings. They were eager to expand such rights to other aspects of their lives. Stanton had participated in a petition campaign to support a recently enacted New York law that gave married women limited rights to inherit and own property. The men who voted for this law were generally not motivated by considerations of gender equity; they sought to protect a woman's inherited property from her husband's debts and shield a couple's assets in a rapidly changing economy.[10] Nevertheless, the law gave married women new legal rights. Stanton's cousin Gerrit Smith had in June become the presidential candidate of the (short-lived) radical antislavery National Liberty Party. At the party's convention in Buffalo, New York, he advocated for universal suffrage. The five women gathered in Seneca Falls likely sensed that a new spirit was abroad in the land.

Although the organizers provided only ten days' notice of the convention, three hundred people packed into the Methodist Wesleyan Chapel, which had been built by a congregation of abolitionists, on July 19 and 20, 1848. Nearly all attendees were from upstate New York, and most were Quakers or Methodists.[11] Both men and women attended, although men were asked to be silent observers during the first day's sessions. Frederick Douglass, the self-emancipated slave who had become a leading abolitionist activist, was present. In a decision that demonstrated how far women would have to go to achieve equality, Lucretia Mott's husband presided during the second day because none of the organizers was prepared to lead a meeting in which both women and men would participate.

At the convention, Stanton presented the "Declaration of Sentiments and Resolutions" that she had drafted in M'Clintock's parlor. Modeled after the nation's Declaration of Independence, the "Declaration of Sentiments" began by asserting that men and women are created equal and then listed a long series of injustices women confronted, including lack of marital rights, unequal wages, inferior education, and the denial of "her inalienable right to the elective franchise." The "Declaration of Sentiments" charged men with direct responsibility for women's subordination and demanded for women

Wesleyan Methodist Church, site of the Seneca Falls Convention. *Courtesy of Alice Berenson.*

Parlor in the M'Clintock House where Stanton drafted the "Declaration of Sentiments." *Courtesy of Alice Berenson.*

"immediate admission to all the rights and privileges which belong to them as citizens of the United States."[12]

Convention delegates unanimously adopted resolutions to grant women equal rights in marriage, at schools, and to jobs and wages. When the debate turned to suffrage, Frederick Douglass spoke in support. He argued that a just government requires the free consent of the governed, and therefore "there can be no reason in the world for denying to woman the exercise of the elective franchise."[13] Suffrage proved the most divisive resolution, and it was the only one not adopted unanimously.[14] At the convention's end, one-third of the attendees signed their names to the "Declaration of Sentiments."

From a modern vantage point, it may be difficult to understand why delegates viewed voting as more radical than the other goals. But in 1848, suffrage was a frontal assault against the prevailing belief in separate spheres. Granting women the vote would require recognizing them as participants in the public sphere. Moreover, woman suffrage threatened to undercut a man's authority as sole head of a household.

Two weeks later, several of the convention's participants organized a second women's rights convention in Rochester, located fifty miles west of Seneca Falls. A woman, Abigail Bush, presided over this meeting, and Stanton, Mott, and M'Clintock were among those who addressed the gathering. Many progressive Quakers attended, including the parents and sister of Susan B. Anthony. (She was 150 miles away working as a teacher.) The Rochester delegates also approved the "Declaration of Sentiments."

Eager to capitalize on the momentum generated by the two conventions, Stanton suggested that organizers hire Lucy Stone to lecture on women's rights. Though this did not occur, Stanton's proposal reflected how far word of Stone's persuasive powers had already spread. Stone and Stanton, joined several years later by Susan B. Anthony, would soon become the dominant trio in the women's rights movement.

Historians continue to debate the significance of the Seneca Falls Convention. The women's rights movement was not born there; it had already been born in Massachusetts. Nor did that meeting launch an organized, national movement. That momentous step would occur two years later in Worcester, Massachusetts.

That Seneca Falls' importance has been exaggerated does not mean that it was inconsequential, however. It was the first convention ever held for the purpose of discussing women's rights. The "Declaration of Sentiments" grounded the embryonic women's movement in the Declaration of Independence's pledge that equality is "self-evident." The breadth of the demands provided a blueprint for the future. The Seneca Falls and Rochester conventions, which received substantial positive coverage in abolitionist papers (and negative coverage in other outlets) likely contributed to the decision of Stone and her Boston colleagues to organize the First National Woman's Rights Convention in Worcester.

THE FIRST NATIONAL WOMAN'S RIGHTS CONVENTION

Following an antislavery convention in Boston in the spring of 1850, Lucy Stone, Abby Kelley Foster, Paulina Wright Davis, and several other women decided to plan the first ever national woman's rights convention.[15] Davis, who lived in Rhode Island, had studied medicine and lectured to women on physiology. A well-off widow committed to both abolitionism and women's rights, she would be the lead organizer and preside at the convention.

Organizers hoped to attract an array of reformers to the cause of women's rights and create a formal structure of committees to carry efforts forward between annual conventions. Allowing plenty of time for planning and publicity, they scheduled the convention to take place six months later in Worcester. Besides being in the hometown county of both Stone and Kelley Foster, Worcester was the state's second-largest city and a key railroad hub that connected Massachusetts to other New England states, the mid-Atlantic and the Midwest.

Eighty-nine women and men signed the Call to the Convention, among them Stone, Kelley Foster, Davis, Stanton, William Lloyd Garrison, and Gerrit Smith. The Call announced that the convention would consider "the great question of Woman's Rights, Duties, and Relations." Organizers reached out to the Grimké sisters and Lucretia Mott, among others, to encourage their participation. "We need all the women who are accustomed to speaking in public—every stick of timber that is sound," pressed Stone.[16]

Organizers hoped that Margaret Fuller, a prominent former Bostonian then living in Italy, would play a key role. A central member of Boston's transcendentalist community, she had also initiated and hosted "conversations" where some of the city's women came together to discuss diverse intellectual subjects, including history and literature. Fuller had published an article about the role of women in American society for the *Dial*, the local transcendentalist journal that she edited from 1840 to 1844. She expanded the article into a book, *Woman in the Nineteenth Century*, published in 1845. Fuller criticized the barriers that circumscribed the paths available to men and women, arguing that they prevented members of both genders from achieving their full potential. Her harshest criticisms were directed at those societal customs and expectations that prevented girls from learning and pursuing careers. "Let [girls] be sea captains if they will," she urged. Sadly, she did not live long enough to attend the Worcester Convention; while returning from Italy, she perished in a shipwreck off the New York coast in July 1850.

In another reminder of the perils of the era, Stone herself nearly did not make it to the convention. She was called away to Illinois, where her brother, Luther, was fatally ill with cholera. On her way home, her brother's widow gave birth to a stillborn son. While caring for her sister-in-law, Stone contracted and nearly died from typhoid fever.

Impressively, close to 1,000 people from eleven states packed into Worcester's Brinley Hall on October 23, 1850. Of the attendees, 267 registered as members, which allowed them voting privileges. Approximately

200 of the registered members hailed from Massachusetts; others came from Connecticut, Maine, New Hampshire, Rhode Island, New York, Ohio, and Pennsylvania.[17]

In her opening address, Paulina Wright Davis urged the assembly to focus on achieving results. "It is one thing to issue a declaration of rights," but quite another "to secure the desired reformation," she announced. When Stone took the floor, she spoke of the "inferior and slavish" position of women and explained that women want "to be something more than the appendages of Society." To great applause, she continued, "We want that when [a woman] dies, it may not be written on her gravestone that she was the 'relict' of somebody." She urged women to circulate petitions demanding suffrage.

Stanton's family responsibilities prevented her from attending, but she sent a letter endorsing the demand for suffrage. Observing that she had never seen "one good reason why one half of the citizens of this Republic have no voice in the laws which govern them," she proceeded to demolish the "bad reasons." To those who argued that a woman's interest in political affairs would destroy "domestic harmony," she retorted that this so-called harmony

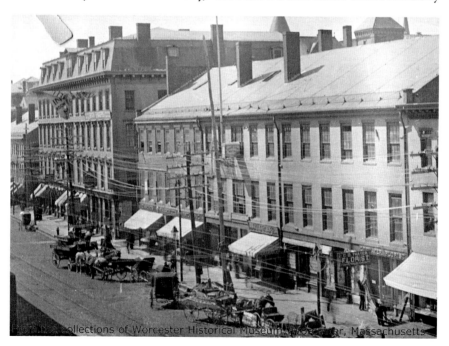

Brinley Hall, Worcester, site of the first National Woman's Rights Convention. *Courtesy of Worcester Historical Museum.*

was in reality subordination. To those who claimed that "refined, delicate" women should not be exposed to "violence and vulgarity" at the polls, she said the presence of women would reduce violence and soften vulgarity. To those who worried that women would next want to hold office, she replied, they would "most certainly."

While the vast majority of attendees were native-born, middle-class, literate, white Protestants, two of the speakers who addressed the Worcester delegates stood out. Sojourner Truth was born a slave in New York in about 1797. She fled slavery in 1826, one year before it was abolished in that state. She adopted the name Sojourner Truth and became an abolitionist and itinerant preacher. She told the audience that if "the treatment of women in this country was a proof of its civilization, the heathen would have to come yet and teach them civilization." Truth would go on to speak at other conventions, including a local one in Akron, Ohio, in 1851, where she delivered her famous "Ain't I a Woman" speech. In response to those who claimed that women were weaker than men and needed their protection, she explained that as a black woman, she performed arduous physical labor and received none of the purported benefits of male chivalry. To claims that Jesus's gender was proof of male superiority, she retorted that he came from "God and a woman."[18]

The other unusual Worcester speaker was Ernestine Rose. The daughter of a rabbi in Poland, she had immigrated to the United States in 1826 at age twenty-six. In New York, Rose rejected organized religion, led a petition drive in support of the Married Women's Property Act, and advocated for the rights of women to equal wages and the vote. In Worcester, she argued that a woman's proper sphere should be determined only by her "powers and capacities, strengthened and refined by an education in accordance with her nature."

The voting members adopted a series of resolutions, including one declaring that every human being "who is required to obey the law, is entitled to a voice in its enactments" and another stating that "women are clearly entitled to the right of suffrage, and to be considered eligible to office." Because voting rights were controlled by individual states, the resolution further demanded that the word "male" be stricken from every state constitution. Consistent with the abolitionist sentiments of the attendees, that resolution also supported suffrage for blacks. It pledged that "every party which claims to represent the humanity, civilization, and progress of the age, is bound to inscribe on its banners, Equality before the law, without distinction of sex or color."

Sojourner Truth. *Courtesy of the Library of Congress.*

Before adjourning, convention delegates appointed eighteen women and men, including Stone, Kelley Foster, and Davis, to serve on a central committee that would plan future annual conventions intended to guide "public opinion upward and onward in the grand social reform of establishing woman's co-sovereignty with man." The convention also created five subcommittees to focus on the discrete areas of "education, industrial avocations, civil and political functions, social relations, and publication."

The radical abolitionist press praised the Worcester convention, but the mainstream press was harshly critical, referring to it as a "Hens' Convention" or an "Insurrection in Petticoats." The *New York Herald* published a particularly scathing review. It called the convention a "motley gathering of fanatical mongrels, of old grannies, male and female, of fugitive slaves and fugitive lunatics" and declared that their proposals, if enacted, would "reduce society to the most beastly and promiscuous confusion." But the adage that no publicity is bad publicity would hold true in these early years: even critical articles helped the cause of women's rights by broadcasting the existence of the growing movement.[19]

A year later, when the Second National Woman's Rights Convention convened in Worcester, the audience was larger. Unable to fit into Brinley Hall, three thousand attendees crowded into Worcester City Hall. Alluding to the hard work that had paved the way for this extraordinary gathering, Abby Kelley Foster told the delegates, "For fourteen years, I have advocated this cause by my daily life. Bloody feet, sisters, have worn smooth the path by which you have come up hither."[20]

Paulina Wright Davis again presided at the 1851 convention. Angelina Grimké attended, and Stanton again sent a letter of support. In her remarks, Lucy Stone compared the stark differences facing a young man and woman as they contemplated adulthood. A young man, she said, regardless how poor or lowly born "looks abroad over the wide world's arena, and sees no height to which he may not aspire; no place of honor which he may not fill." But his sister, she lamented, finds her aspirations limited to the schoolhouse, the chair of the seamstress, and household drudgery. "Once you have mentioned those, you have marked the limit of woman's aspiration." Stone urged women not to ask, "give us this, or give us that," but instead to "just get up and take it." The convention proceedings noted that her statement was met with "loud cheers."

Reflecting the degree to which activists had coalesced in support of suffrage, the convention's first resolution asserted, "That while we would not undervalue other methods, the Right of Suffrage for Woman is, in our opinion, the cornerstone of this enterprise, since we do not seek to protect woman, but rather to place her in a position to protect herself."

Wishing to reach more people in other regions, the central committee selected Syracuse, an abolitionist stronghold in upstate New York, as the location for the Third National Woman's Rights Convention. Notably, Susan B. Anthony would attend this 1852 gathering. Lucy Stone's speech there is generally credited with persuading Anthony to dedicate her energy to the women's rights movement.

Anthony was born in the western Massachusetts town of Adams in 1820; when she was six, her family moved to upstate New York, ultimately settling in Rochester. Like the daughters of many reform-minded Quaker families, she became a schoolteacher and worked as head of the girls' division of Canajoharie Academy in upstate New York. She also became active in the local temperance movement, and she delivered her first public speech at a gathering of the Daughters of Temperance in 1849.

The temperance movement was another product of the Great Awakening. This movement, which focused on the social ills that resulted from excessive alcohol consumption, also offered women an opportunity to look outward and seek to improve society. When Anthony returned to Rochester in 1849, she continued her involvement in the temperance movement while embracing the abolitionist and women's rights causes. Considered unflappable and dignified, Anthony would prove to be an effective leader and organizer.

Anthony had met her future ally Stanton in Seneca Falls in 1851. They were introduced by reformer Amelia Bloomer, who had attended the Seneca Falls Convention. Bloomer is best remembered today for urging women to wear clothing that was more practical and comfortable than the tight-laced dresses typically worn by middle- and upper-class women of that era. Her eponymous bloomer consisted of a corsetless, knee-length dress and baggy pants. As might be expected, Stone wore a bloomer to the 1852 convention. The apparel met with such widespread derision from both men and women, however, that it was quickly abandoned as an unnecessary distraction from the movement's goals.

The women's rights conventions of 1853–56 were held in Cleveland, Philadelphia, Cincinnati, and New York City, respectively. Between conventions, Stone maintained a grueling travel schedule as she lectured both for women's rights and against slavery. Though her speeches were sometimes met with scorn, she became a popular speaker on the lyceum circuit. She was able to command substantial speaking fees and donated a portion of them to help sustain the women's movement. Demonstrating the nation's growing interest in both Stone and the movement, impresario P.T. Barnum unsuccessfully sought to hire her for a lecture tour.[21]

As part of her efforts, Stone tried to reform Massachusetts state laws to make them more favorable to women. In 1853, Massachusetts held a state constitutional convention.[22] She and her allies hoped to persuade delegates to strike the word *male* from the state's voting qualifications. In preparation, Stone delivered dozens of lectures and gathered 2,000 signatures on petitions. The Massachusetts Senate Committee on Voter Qualifications agreed to hear from the petitioners, and she appeared before it, along with abolitionist and women's rights backer Wendell Phillips. But the committee refused to act. Observing that only 2,000 of 200,000 women of voting age had made the request, the committee concluded that the vast proportion of the women of Massachusetts were content with the status quo.[23]

Susan B. Anthony. *Courtesy of the Library of Congress.*

This decision foreshadowed a difficulty that would plague the woman suffrage movement for decades. Repeatedly, opponents would assert that women should be enfranchised only when a majority of them demanded the ballot. Suffrage supporters would indignantly retort that inalienable rights do not require majority support. Stone and other advocates knew, however, that they had to raise the consciousness of women and make them resent their subordinate status.

Stone additionally advocated for repeal of coverture laws, which suspended the legal existence of women during marriage. This effort proved more successful. In 1855, Massachusetts enacted a law permitting married women to own and sell property, control their earnings, and make wills.

During these years, Stone, Anthony, and Stanton became close collaborators. The three had met together for the first time in 1852, when Stanton invited them, along with abolitionist newspaper editor Horace Greeley, to Seneca Falls. Anthony and Stanton began their legendary partnership when they together lobbied the New York legislature to expand the rights granted to married women. Their efforts culminated in an 1860 law that gave women important new rights, including control of their own earnings and joint guardianship over children.

Anthony and Stone were also regular collaborators. Besides working together to organize women's rights conventions, they joined forces in the abolitionist movement. They shared the experience, then unusual for women, of travel and lecturing.[24] Their letters reflected their close friendship. They were also determined to remain unmarried. But while Anthony would remain single, Stone married her tenacious suitor Henry Browne Blackwell in 1855. From a reformist family, he was an abolitionist, and his sister, Elizabeth, had in 1849 become the first woman in America to earn a medical degree.

The newlyweds used their marriage ceremony to make a political statement. They issued a "Protest" announcing their opposition to laws "that refuse to recognize a wife as an independent, rational being, while they confer upon the husband an injurious and unnatural superiority, investing him with legal powers which no honorable man would exercise, and which no man should possess." Stone also retained her maiden name, a radical decision without precedent.

Annual women's rights conventions continued for the remainder of the 1850s, except in 1857. Stone, who was by then living in New Jersey, had recently given birth to her daughter, Alice Stone Blackwell. The financial panic of 1857, coupled with Stone's inability to travel to earn lecture fees, led to a shortage of funds. Conventions resumed the following year and were held in New York City from 1858 to 1860.

Stone, who was thirty-nine when Alice was born, largely withdrew from public lecturing for a time. Those years were sorrowfully punctuated by the death of a premature newborn in 1858 and of her mother in 1860. Stone was hardly silent, however. In 1858, she wrote to the tax collector in New Jersey that she refused to pay her property tax bill because "women suffer taxation and yet have no representation, which is not only unjust to one half of the adult population, but is contrary to our theory of government."[25] In response, officials seized a portion of the family property and sold it at auction, but supporters purchased and returned it.

Tensions between Stone and Stanton first developed around the convention held in May 1860. They had never developed as close a bond as Anthony had with each of them. In contrast to Stone, whose past was marked by her struggles to earn an education and a living, Stanton was from a privileged background. Stone was also self-effacing, while Stanton was "boldly confident."[26] Stanton wanted the convention to consider reforms to permit divorce in cases of desertion, cruelty, or drunkenness. Stone, who did not attend the convention, refused to give her support. She knew that detractors called any proposed liberalization of grounds for divorce "free love" and used this to paint women's rights activists as immoral radicals determined to overthrow the social order. Their disagreement portended future frictions.[27]

Still, the 1850s were very successful for the pioneers of the women's movement. Conventions brought together thousands of reformers. Married women achieved new legal rights in nine northern and midwestern states. Activists' demands for the ballot became routine. Many journalists came to regard the subject of women's rights as worthy of serious reporting. Because women contributed enormously to the abolitionist effort, they had powerful allies within the new, antislavery Republican Party.

Conventions and discussions about women's rights were suspended following the presidential election in November 1860. War over the future of slavery became imminent when southern states responded to the election of Republican Abraham Lincoln by seceding from the Union and forming the Confederate States of America. Four bloody years followed, during which women assumed many new roles. When the war ended in a Union victory that eradicated slavery, there appeared the possibility that the franchise would be expanded to include both African Americans and women. This glittering hope would soon be dashed. In the process, the women's rights movement would split into two warring camps.

3

WAR AND SCHISM

The Civil War years proved to be a transformative era for women. They served as nurses, worked in factories, and managed farms and businesses. Many thousands volunteered in support of the efforts of the Sanitary Commission, a private relief agency that raised millions of dollars to provision active troops and aid ill and injured soldiers. Several hundred even disguised themselves as men and enlisted to fight. Clara Barton, a Massachusetts native who served as a nurse and later founded the American Red Cross, observed that the war years advanced women "at least fifty years…[beyond] the normal position which continued peace would have assigned her."[1] These broad gains would help the cause of women's rights only over the long run, however. When war began, leading women activists suspended their work on behalf of women's rights. Instead, they joined other abolitionists in supporting the Union war effort and persuading President Lincoln to issue a proclamation ending slavery.

The leading triumvirate of Anthony, Stanton, and Stone remained allies during the war years. Stone continued to live in New Jersey, focusing most of her energy on her young daughter. Her financial worries were reduced in 1864, when her husband's real estate speculations paid off and he largely retired from his business endeavors. Stanton and her family moved to New York City in 1861 when her husband was appointed deputy collector of the Port of New York. Anthony spent much of her time in that city as well, frequently staying with Stanton. Their friendship flourished.

Abraham Lincoln took a momentous step toward ending slavery when he issued the Emancipation Proclamation on January 1, 1863. Abolitionists then turned their attention to seeking a constitutional amendment that would guarantee slavery's extinction. Anthony and Stanton organized the Women's Loyal National League to support this campaign. Anthony nominated Stone to preside at the league's first convention in May 1863, where attendees organized a petition drive that Anthony led. The league collected 400,000 signatures before disbanding in 1864, when it became clear that Congress would approve the Thirteenth Amendment abolishing slavery.

Abolitionists then set their sights on enfranchising black men. The Emancipation Proclamation had allowed black men to join the Union army, and nearly 200,000 black men were serving in the Union army or navy. At a convention of black men held in October 1864, Frederick Douglass and others argued: "Are we good enough to use bullets and not good enough to use ballots?...May we give our lives, but not our votes, for the good of the republic?"[2] When the Civil War ended in Union victory in April 1865, Douglass told the Massachusetts Anti-Slavery Society that the time was ripe to press for this foundational right of citizenship.[3]

At the same time, Stone, Anthony, and Stanton prepared to move forward on women's rights and, in particular, on suffrage. The three believed that their male abolitionist allies would support universal suffrage—that is, the enfranchisement of both blacks and women. After all, Douglass had included women in his plea for suffrage, announcing that "my heart and my voice go with the movement to extend suffrage to woman."[4]

The three leaders became worried, however, when leading Boston abolitionist Wendell Phillips announced it was "the Negro's hour." Woman suffrage must wait, he asserted, until after black male suffrage was secured. Pragmatic political concerns likely motivated Phillips's declaration, which would ultimately be endorsed by most other leading male abolitionists. They were focused on their plans to reconstruct the South in a fashion that would guarantee rights to the formerly enslaved. Newly enfranchised blacks would undoubtedly support the Republican Party and enhance its political clout. Women's votes, in contrast, would likely mirror the diverse affiliations of the overall population. Further, many abolitionists argued that black men's military service made them more deserving of suffrage than women and that adding the radical issue of woman suffrage to their postwar agenda might derail progress on race relations. Many no doubt believed that women should remain in their traditional sphere.

The woman suffragists grew anxious in late 1865 when Congress considered a proposed Fourteenth Amendment. Section 1 of the proposed amendment, which would confer citizenship on all persons born or naturalized in the United States, was gender neutral.[5] But Section 2 of the proposed amendment would, for the first time, introduce gender distinctions into the Constitution. That section would penalize states in proportion to the extent they withheld the vote from any male inhabitants.

Frederick Douglass. Original image located at the Art Institute of Chicago. *Public domain.*

In response, Anthony, Stone, and Stanton jointly wrote to past supporters of woman suffrage. "As the question of Suffrage is now agitating the public mind, it is the hour for Woman to make her demand," their letter declared. They urged women "unitedly" to petition for the right to vote.[6]

In May 1866, as Congress was on the verge of adopting the Fourteenth Amendment, Anthony and Stanton convened the Eleventh National Women's Rights Convention in New York City. (Stone did not attend this convention.) The Call to Convention warned that the amendment, which would secure suffrage "but to another shade of manhood," would not bring the nation "one line nearer the republican idea" of equal rights to all.[7]

Frances Ellen Watkins Harper, a black woman who had been a leader in Philadelphia's abolitionist community, was among the speakers to call for universal suffrage. A published poet and mother of four, she related how, after her husband's death two years earlier, the government had seized all of her property to pay his debts. Had she died instead, she reminded the audience, "no administrator would have gone into his house, broken up his home, and sold his bed." Harper called particular attention to the plight of black women in language that emphasized what is today called the "intersectionality" of gender and racial discrimination. "You white women speak here of rights," she stated, "I speak of wrongs. I as a colored woman have had in this country an education which has made me feel as if I were in the situation of Ishmael, my hand against every man, and every man's hand against me."[8]

Convention participants adopted a new, inclusive strategy. They transformed themselves into a new association, the American Equal Rights

Association (AERA), dedicated to securing "equal rights to all American citizens, especially the right of suffrage, irrespective of race, color, or sex." Stone, Anthony, and Stanton were all elected to the executive committee, and Lucretia Mott was selected as president.

While the Fourteenth Amendment was pending, Stone, Stanton, and Anthony tried to persuade several states to amend their state constitutions to enfranchise women. Success would provide momentum to their campaign for a federal amendment guaranteeing universal suffrage. They argued their case before a subcommittee of the New York State Constitutional Convention, but their efforts failed. Stone made a similar, also unsuccessful argument before the New Jersey legislature.

The three then focused their energies on Kansas, where the state's white male voters were to vote on two referenda in November 1867. The first referendum would strike "white" from the list of voter qualifications; the second would strike "male" from that list. The support for the two referenda differed dramatically, however. The state's Republican Party believed this was "the Negro's hour" and refused to campaign for the woman suffrage amendment.

The schism that would soon divide Lucy Stone from Susan B. Anthony and Elizabeth Cady Stanton began in Kansas. Stone and her husband campaigned there in support of both referenda despite their anger at the state Republican Party for refusing to support woman suffrage. But Anthony and Stanton took a different approach. Incensed at the state's Republicans, the two entered into an alliance with George Francis Train, an openly racist, wealthy Democrat. "Woman first, and Negro last, is my programme," he announced.[9] Anthony, Stanton, and Train campaigned together in support of woman suffrage but not black male suffrage.

Making matters worse from Stone's point of view, Anthony and Stanton continued their alliance with Train even after Kansas defeated both referenda by wide margins (though black suffrage had fared better than woman suffrage among voters). Train joined Anthony and Stanton on a lecture tour as they traveled back to New York. Horrified, Stone wrote that these joint lectures were held "without consultation or approval" of the American Equal Rights Association, which "disclaims all responsibility for or endorsement of" the lectures. She refused to permit the AERA to reimburse Anthony and Stanton for their Kansas expenses. Stone and her husband additionally accused Anthony of improper accounting and misspending AERA funds.[10]

In the face of criticism, Anthony and Stanton became defensive. Rather than ending their relationship with Train, they strengthened it. They decided to publish a newspaper in New York City in support of woman suffrage that Train would finance. The first issue of the *Revolution* appeared on January 8, 1868. Demonstrating the race-based tension that was already fracturing the woman suffrage movement, the *Revolution* announced it would advocate for "educated suffrage, irrespective of sex or color," a clear reference to prioritizing suffrage for white women over that for black men.[11]

Historians have struggled to explain why Anthony and Stanton were willing to embrace a racist Democrat and antagonize former allies. One possible reason is that New York legislators had in 1862 repealed some of the rights women had won only two years earlier, including a mother's right to equal guardianship of children and a widow's right to control property left at death for the care of minor children. That experience reinforced the necessity of the ballot to hold legislators accountable. Anthony and Stanton also may have realized that a postwar window in which to achieve radical change would likely stay open only a short while before it slammed shut.

Additionally, Train offered critically needed financial support for women's rights at a time when former abolitionist allies had not only prioritized black male suffrage but also denied the financially struggling women's movement funds bequeathed to them. An $8,000 per year bequest from a deceased abolitionist stipulated that the money should be used for other reforms, including women's rights, if slavery was abolished before the full bequest was spent. But even after the Thirteenth Amendment was ratified, Wendell Phillips, the chair of the trustee committee, claimed the bequest for the abolitionist movement. He argued that slavery would not be fully abolished until newly freed slaves were enfranchised.[12]

It's also been noted that Stanton frequently argued in the alternative; for example, "I seek universal suffrage, but if that is denied, women deserve suffrage before black men."[13] Moreover, Stanton and Anthony both later reconciled with Frederick Douglass, which might suggest he understood their embrace of Train as more opportunistic than genuine. Other antislavery activists also employed racist arguments for arguably strategic purposes. Henry Blackwell did so in 1867, for instance, when he wrote a pamphlet informing white southerners that the North was "immovably fixed" on black male suffrage. He suggested that because white women would be far more likely to vote than black women, enfranchising women would benefit the political agenda of southern whites. His wife's reaction is unknown.[14]

Relations among the former friends and allies further deteriorated in July 1868, the same month the Fourteenth Amendment was ratified. Anthony and Stanton announced the formation of a new organization, the Woman's

Suffrage Association of America, with the *Revolution* as its organ. The four-member central committee included Anthony and Stanton but not Stone. That same month, Stanton wrote in the *Revolution*, "We protest against the enfranchisement of another man of any race or clime until the daughters of Jefferson, Hancock, and Adams are crowned with all their rights." That fall, she further incensed her former Republican allies by publicly praising Frank Blair, the openly racist Democratic nominee for vice president.[15]

In reaction, a group of New England women still closely allied with Republican abolitionists, including Abby Kelley Foster, formed a separate organization. The New England Woman Suffrage Association (NEWSA) resolved to advocate for a constitutional amendment "extending suffrage to all men and women as the inalienable birthright of every American citizen."[16] Julia Ward Howe was elected president. She had become a national celebrity during the Civil War when she wrote "Battle Hymn of the Republic." Stone, who would soon move from New Jersey to Boston, addressed NEWSA's inaugural meeting in November 1868 and was selected to serve on its executive committee. Stanton and Anthony, both New Yorkers, were not invited. In an unmistakable challenge to the *Revolution*, NEWSA began its own newspaper, the *Woman's Advocate*.

The crack between the New Englanders and the New Yorkers widened in the final weeks of 1868, when the first drafts of the Fifteenth Amendment began to circulate in Congress. This proposed amendment would grant suffrage to all men and prohibit both the federal and state governments from denying or abridging the vote based on "race, color, or previous condition of servitude." Women were omitted. This was no accidental oversight. Republican Ulysses S. Grant had recently won the presidency with 52.7 percent of the vote. Black men in the South had carried him to victory in several states in the former Confederacy, and Republicans were anxious to increase and preserve their party's strength as the remaining former Confederate states rejoined the Union. Adding southern women's votes to the tally would put the party at risk.

Julia Ward Howe. *Public domain.*

Stanton reacted to the amendment with alarm—and racist appeals. She wrote in the *Revolution* that "if woman finds it hard to bear the oppressive law of a few Saxon fathers…what may she not be called to endure when all the lower orders, natives and foreigners, Dutch, Irish, Chinese and African, legislate for her and her daughters?" She accused American politicians of degrading their own mothers, wives, and daughters "below unwashed and unlettered ditch-diggers, boot-blacks, hostlers, butchers, and barbers." She even connected black male suffrage to sexual assault, a longstanding racist tactic, writing that enfranchising black men but not women would "create an antagonism between black men and all women that will culminate in fearful outrages on womanhood, especially in the southern states."[17]

In February 1869, Congress approved the Fifteenth Amendment and sent it to the states for ratification. The next month, Congressman George Washington Julian of Indiana introduced a proposed Sixteenth Amendment that would prohibit the denial of suffrage based on gender. This amendment stalled in Congress, however.

The American Equal Rights Association would now have to decide at its upcoming meeting, scheduled for May 1869, whether to support the Fifteenth Amendment despite the absence of any clause enfranchising women. What has been called "one of the saddest divorces in American history" occurred at that meeting, which drew over a thousand attendees to Steinway Hall in New York City.[18] When Stanton announced that she would not support "Patrick and Sambo and Hans and Yung Tung" making laws for educated white women, Frederick Douglass issued a sharp retort. "I must say I do not see how anyone can pretend that there is the same urgency in giving the ballot to woman as to the Negro," he said. The ballot for black men is a "question of life and death," he continued, because they are the "objects of insult and outrage at every turn" and live in fear of being "dragged from their houses and hung upon lamp-posts." Undeterred, Anthony countered that "if intelligence, justice, and morality are to have precedence in government, let the question of women be brought up first and that of the Negro last."[19]

Stone took the floor to defend the claims of both women and blacks. "Woman has an ocean of wrongs too deep for any plummet," she stated, "and the Negro, too, has an ocean of wrongs that cannot be fathomed." She expressed her deep unhappiness that the Fifteenth Amendment excluded women, whom she said would do more than black men to promote "an element of restoration and harmony." Nevertheless, she "thank[ed] God for that Fifteenth Amendment." She explained, "I will be thankful in my soul if anybody can get out of the terrible pit."[20]

Even before the divisive meeting concluded, Anthony and Stanton invited their supporters—pointedly excluding Stone—to a private meeting where they formed a new organization, the National Woman Suffrage Association (NWSA). Stanton became president, while Anthony headed the executive committee. Only women were permitted to serve as NWSA officers. NWSA promptly passed a resolution opposing the Fifteenth Amendment.[21] It committed itself to securing a federal woman suffrage amendment and other women's rights reforms, including divorce laws more favorable to women.

Several weeks later, Stone and her allies announced their intention to form a rival organization, the American Woman Suffrage Association (AWSA). AWSA, which would be headquartered in Boston, would support ratification of the Fifteenth Amendment while campaigning for woman suffrage. Thus, unlike NWSA, AWSA began by opposing both gender and racial discrimination.

To demonstrate broad-based northern support (in contrast to the New York–focused NWSA), AWSA was officially formed in November 1869 at a convention held in Cleveland and attended by delegates from twenty-one states. AWSA decided to permit men to hold leadership positions. That decision, they felt, enhanced its ability to reach male voters, who controlled whether to grant women the ballot. Lucy Stone was selected to chair the executive committee, which was charged with managing the business of the organization. The esteemed abolitionist and woman suffrage advocate Reverend Henry Ward Beecher became president; his role was to preside over meetings. Beecher, the brother of author Harriet Beecher Stowe and anti-suffragist Catharine Beecher, had a national reputation; he had been selected by President Abraham Lincoln to deliver the principal oration when the American flag was raised at Fort Sumter following the Confederacy's surrender.

Though neither Sojourner Truth nor Frances Harper attended the founding AWSA convention, they supported the primacy of the Fifteenth Amendment. Harper would address AWSA conventions in 1873 and 1875. Truth sought to avoid entanglement in the rivalry between the two associations, but her loyalty "came finally to rest with AWSA."[22]

Unlike the small, centralized NWSA, AWSA created a decentralized structure. The national organization was intended to nurture and support auxiliary state associations, which would in turn nurture and support auxiliary local associations. The goals listed in AWSA's constitution included forming auxiliary state associations in every state where none existed, cooperating with existing ones, supplying state and local associations with written materials, circulating petitions, employing lecturers and agents, and holding one or more national conventions each year. Each state association was permitted to send as many delegates as it had U.S. congressional representatives to AWSA conventions.[23]

As for its goals, AWSA elected to concentrate on woman suffrage. The vote would give women the tools to remedy other discriminatory laws, its leaders reasoned. Suffrage would also serve as a gateway, they believed, to higher education and the professions. Practical reasons also lay behind this decision. AWSA did not want members to be distracted or divided by other issues. As long as its members supported suffrage, they could agree to disagree over other issues, including "theology, temperance, marriage, race, dress, finance, labor and capital." "As advocates of equal rights," wrote Henry Blackwell, "we protest against loading the good ship Woman Suffrage with a cargo of irrelevant opinion."[24]

Other women's issues would not be ignored, however. Lucy Stone and her husband began the *Woman's Journal* newspaper, which was published weekly in Boston beginning on January 8, 1870. They were also the largest shareholders in the joint stock company that owned it. The first issue announced its mission: it was "devoted to the interests of Woman, to her educational, industrial, legal and political Equality, and especially to her right to Suffrage." The *Woman's Journal* immediately became a crucial source of both information and communication among AWSA-affiliated suffrage associations. Though not the organ "of any association," it was, Stone announced, "thoroughly identified with the interests and in harmony with the principles of the AWSA."[25] (The *Woman's Journal* absorbed the *Woman's Advocate*, the newspaper started by the New England Woman Suffrage Association the previous year.)

The *Woman's Journal* also adopted a positive outlook; throughout the long suffrage struggle, it would stress progress and maintain that success was inevitable. By celebrating women's achievements in other fields, it also encouraged women across a diverse nation to break down the barriers of laws and customs that held them back.

Mary Livermore, a suffragist and temperance advocate whom Stone had recruited from Chicago, served as the first editor-in-chief. When she resigned in 1872 to become a full-time lecturer, Stone and her husband led the paper. The *Woman's Journal* would be published for more than fifty years. In contrast, the *Revolution* developed financial difficulties almost immediately

Mary Livermore. *Public domain.*

after Train journeyed to Britain and was arrested for supporting Irish revolutionaries. Anthony was forced to sell the *Revolution* in 1870, and it folded in 1872.

When the Fifteenth Amendment was ratified in March 1870, the rift between NWSA and AWSA might have been healed. After all, the success of that amendment left both organizations focused primarily on the same next objective: obtaining a federal amendment enfranchising women. But the schism continued. Stone, Stanton, and Anthony each had a strong personality and iron will, and extreme personal bitterness now divided Stone from Anthony and Stanton. They also disagreed over the scope of the next effort. In January 1871, the *Woman's Journal* advocated "the union of all the friends of woman suffrage, who are able and willing to work together in harmony for the common good without complicating the main question with side issues or compromising it with entangling alliances."[26] But Stanton in particular tied suffrage directly to broader changes in gender relations. Important differences in tactics also quickly became apparent. Twenty long, divisive, and challenging years would pass before the elderly trio would agree to reunite their rival organizations.

4
DECADES OF DIVISION

The years following ratification of the Fifteenth Amendment were frustrating and disappointing for the woman suffrage movement. Not only did the movement face a new conservative climate, but the schism hurt, as the Boston-based American Woman Suffrage Association (AWSA) and the New York–based National Woman Suffrage Association (NWSA) competed for members and financial support. The woman suffrage movement also remained largely populated by a small slice of white, native-born, educated Protestant women. Suffrage leaders seldom found common ground with the many women who struggled daily against prejudice and poverty.

Once slavery was abolished, a conservative "season of reaction" set in.[1] Republican-led Reconstruction of the former Confederacy ended in 1877, and white Democrats took control of the South. The Republican Party in the North turned its energy away from race relations and toward economic growth through increased industrialization—and toward restoring economic ties to the South. Herbert Spencer's philosophy of Social Darwinism, which dominated the postwar decades, posited that Charles Darwin's theories of natural selection and survival of the fittest applied to human society as well as to the natural world. Social Darwinism decreed that societies prospered when the fittest were allowed to compete unfettered by government regulation and labor unions. The result was an era of large corporations and enormous fortunes that Mark Twain aptly named the Gilded Age.

Few Democrats, meanwhile, had an interest in woman suffrage, a reform they associated with radical Republicans. (Train had been an unusual exception.) The Democratic Party's diverse—and sometimes overlapping—constituencies included southern whites, northerners who had opposed the antislavery movement, immigrants, and the industrial working class. In the North, economic class and ethnicity were the flashpoints and basis for partisan divide.

Despite women's expanded roles during the Civil War, the conservative doctrine of gender-based separate spheres flourished anew after the war. The daily division between the worlds of men and women grew larger amid rapid industrialization and urbanization. Fewer couples worked together on family farms and in small rural businesses. Urban-dwelling men generally left home each morning to toil in the worlds of work and politics. Gilded Age traditionalists maintained that home must be a man's refuge presided over by a woman who was pious, pure, domestic, and submissive.[2]

The U.S. Supreme Court endorsed the separate spheres creed in 1872 in a case holding that the Fourteenth Amendment did not grant women the right to practice law. Justice Joseph Bradley, in a concurring opinion joined by two other justices, declared:

> *The natural and proper timidity and delicacy which belongs to the female sex evidently unfits it for many of the occupations of civil life. The Constitution of the family organization, which is founded in the divine ordinance as well as in the nature of things, indicates the domestic sphere as that which properly belongs to the domain and functions of womanhood.... The paramount destiny and mission of woman are to fulfill the noble and benign offices of wife and mother. This is the law of the Creator.[3]*

Conservatives used "science" to bolster their circumscribed views of women. Harvard Medical School professor Edward Clarke claimed that a woman's ovaries shriveled in response to intellectual exertion. Other scientists contended that the generally smaller circumference of women's heads proved their intellectual inferiority.[4] As viewed through the lens of Social Darwinism, women were physically and intellectually inferior to men but possessed natural moral and nurturing abilities well suited to motherhood and homemaking.

Many women agreed that inherent gender differences made voting an unsuitable activity for women. Sarah Josepha Hale, the editor of *Godey's Lady's Book*, the most influential women's magazine of the era, believed that

"The Age of Iron. Man as he expects to be." This Currier & Ives lithograph reflects the fear of many that enfranchising women would reverse gender roles. The husband is home watching the baby and sewing, while his wife leaves in a carriage driven by a woman. A male servant does laundry. *Courtesy of the Library of Congress.*

"God has given to man authority, to woman influence."[5] Hale, who also penned "Mary Had a Little Lamb," believed that suffrage would degrade women and destroy their moral influence by placing them in the midst of real-world political conflicts. She and many other influential women who shared her views did, however, support women's education. Like Catharine Beecher, they wished women to be well prepared for the "profession" of domesticity.

The rival NWSA and AWSA persevered during these challenging postwar decades. NWSA devoted itself to seeking a federal amendment enfranchising women. AWSA sought the same goal but believed it was impractical to seek a federal amendment before the proper foundation was laid. It therefore dedicated itself to the labor-intensive work of building support through campaigns for state suffrage. Regardless of their chosen strategies, however, both organizations had a long uphill climb in a hostile environment. There is no better way to illuminate the atmosphere during these decades of schism than beginning with NWSA's early, unfortunate alliance with Victoria Woodhull.

THE NATIONAL WOMAN SUFFRAGE ASSOCIATION

Though headquartered in New York City, NWSA held its annual meetings in Washington, D.C., because its focus was persuading Congress to adopt a federal woman suffrage amendment. Hopeful that legislators would be sympathetic to direct pleas from woman suffragists, Anthony and Stanton sought to convince Congress to hear from advocates. In what would turn out to be a disastrous decision, they endorsed the efforts of Victoria Woodhull.

A fortuneteller and spiritualist, Woodhull had become a wealthy stockbroker in New York with the assistance of railroad industrialist Cornelius Vanderbilt, who reportedly had an extramarital affair with her sister. The sisters founded a newspaper, *Woodhull & Claflin's Weekly*. The House Judiciary Committee permitted Woodhull to testify in support of woman suffrage in 1871. Advancing a "New Departure" theory favored by some NWSA members, Woodhull argued that the Fourteenth Amendment had implicitly enfranchised women by granting them the "privileges and immunities" of citizenship. Though Congress did not act, Anthony and Stanton praised Woodhull's efforts.

Accusations of sexual scandal soon surrounded Woodhull, however. She and her husband shared their home with her ex-husband, who was disabled. Her newspaper supported "sexual self-determination." By this, she meant the right of a woman to "love whom I may…[for] as long or as short a period as I can; to change that love every day if I please."[6] But American women of the Victorian era were not supposed to publicly acknowledge—or even have—sexual feelings. When Woodhull was roundly condemned for endorsing what the press called "free love," she struck back at the many she deemed hypocrites. She targeted in particular Reverend Henry Ward Beecher, the esteemed president of AWSA, who was among those who had denounced her.

Woodhull published an article claiming that Beecher was having an adulterous affair with one of his parishioners. The scandal captivated the nation and spurred on those who claimed the suffrage movement was populated by social extremists. The thirty-four-year-old Woodhull then provocatively declared herself a candidate for the U.S. presidency in November 1872. She became the nominee of the short-lived Equal Rights Party formed by a small, radical faction within NWSA. Her name did not appear on the ballot in any state.

Anthony belatedly banished Woodhull and took tight control of NWSA. Having learned her lesson, Anthony would thereafter focus NWSA on suffrage, although Stanton continued to press for broader reforms. But much damage had been done, and more was still to come. The parishioner's husband sued Beecher on civil charges of adultery, and the trial, which was filled with scandalous details, was a news sensation. Though jurors were unable to reach a verdict, the negative publicity this affair brought to the woman suffrage movement was a political disaster. NWSA's already small membership declined precipitously.[7] But AWSA, too, was severely affected, as will be discussed later.

After banishing Woodhull, Anthony turned to a direct-action strategy based on the assertion that the Fourteenth Amendment had already enfranchised women. In an approach that, helpfully, demanded little organization and few resources, Anthony and a number of supporters showed up at polling stations on November 5, 1872, and attempted to vote. If arrested, they asserted that the Fourteenth Amendment had conferred citizenship and its attendant rights on women. This was not a completely new strategy. Lucy Stone, for example, had attempted to vote in New Jersey in 1868. But NWSA intended to bring the issue before the courts. Anthony was among those arrested. Following a trial, she was convicted and fined $100. She had no opportunity to appeal because the trial judge took no action to collect the fine.

The U.S. Supreme Court soon considered the appeal of Virginia Minor of Missouri, who had attempted to register to vote. The court ruled that neither the Fourteenth Amendment nor any other provision of the U.S. Constitution enfranchised women.

Though it failed as a legal strategy, Anthony's trial and her related New York speaking tour elevated her prominence. She remained in the public eye as she traveled and lectured throughout the nation. She also came to realize the necessity of state suffrage campaigns and adopted AWSA's strategy of organizing state suffrage associations and supporting state campaigns. In 1881, a small NWSA chapter even formed in AWSA's home state of Massachusetts.

Anthony's and Stanton's efforts also included what is perhaps their most enduring contribution during the twenty-year schism: they wrote and published the first three volumes of a "history" of the woman suffrage movement. They had dual motivations for this ambitious undertaking. They wished to record the early years of the movement for future generations, but they also sought to mold historical memory to their own benefit. In this venture, they were joined by Matilda Joslyn Gage, a member of NWSA's executive committee.

Anthony and Stanton invited Stone to report on AWSA, but she declined, stating she had "neither the time nor inclination to write personal sketches of ourselves or the history of what we have done while the work [of suffrage] remains unfinished." She also doubted the good faith of her rivals, contending, "your 'wing' surely are not competent to write the history of 'our wing.'"[8]

When Harriot Stanton Blatch, Stanton's daughter, learned that Anthony and her mother intended to ignore AWSA, she insisted on adding one chapter about that organization. Even so, Blatch's effort was limited to a dry summary of AWSA convention proceedings. She conveyed little of AWSA's extensive activities and influence. That chapter dangles as an afterthought at the end of the second volume.

The first two volumes of *History of Woman Suffrage*, published in 1881 and 1882, covered the years through 1876. The third volume, published in 1886, extended the story through 1885.[9] These volumes were as biased and incomplete as Stone had feared. Anthony and Stanton crafted a narrative that placed them at the forefront, omitted or curtailed embarrassing episodes, and minimized the roles of their rivals. No one reading *History of Woman Suffrage* would realize that AWSA was the more vital suffrage association during the 1870s, for example. The book elevated Anthony and Stanton to the Mount Olympus of the suffrage movement, where they remain today.

History of Woman Suffrage also made Seneca Falls the birthplace of the suffrage movement, a position it retains today. This was contrary to what even NWSA had acknowledged until that point. Like other suffragists, NWSA had recognized the Worcester Convention as the original launch of the organized woman suffrage movement. Admitting the central place of the Worcester Convention had become problematic for Anthony and Stanton, however. Neither had attended it. By contrast, Stanton had played a leading role at Seneca Falls. Anthony had not been at Seneca Falls, either, but she hailed from nearby Rochester. Stone, meanwhile, had no connection to Seneca Falls or upstate New York.

Anthony and Stanton also crafted a legend concerning the impetus for the Seneca Falls Convention that even today is rarely questioned. They claimed that the idea was hatched in 1840, when Stanton and Lucretia Mott met in London at the Anti-Slavery Convention, where delegates had excluded women from participating. Mott, however, did not recall that memory. The less dramatic truth is almost certainly that the idea for a convention was first envisioned when Mott visited Seneca Falls eight years later. The legend, however, permitted NWSA to claim its origins in gender discrimination within the antislavery movement in contrast to AWSA, which was undeniably rooted in an alliance with the antislavery movement.[10]

Stone displayed her frustration in the *Woman's Journal*. She wrote that *History of Woman Suffrage* was premature; it was, she remarked, as if abolitionists had written a history of their movement while slaves still toiled on southern plantations. She reiterated her claim of bias, stating "the editors of this book are not in a position to write fairly on the work of a large class of Suffragists, from whose methods of work, during the last dozen years, their own have widely differed."[11]

THE AMERICAN WOMAN SUFFRAGE ASSOCIATION

Because the self-effacing Stone and her allies never wrote a competing account of their own work, the vital work of AWSA still remains largely unheralded and unfamiliar. Contrary to the accusation of NWSA, repeated by many historians,[12] AWSA also sought a federal amendment enfranchising women. Its members believed, however, that persuading a number of states to enfranchise women was a necessary prerequisite. Congress was unlikely to act until a critical mass of senators and representatives were beholden to women voters in their home states. Moreover, even if Congress were to propose an amendment, ratification by three-quarters of the state legislatures was required. AWSA recognized that success would, therefore, require the labor-intensive work of changing public opinion through a series of exhausting and often unsuccessful state campaigns. AWSA members took the long view, realizing that losing campaigns would have to be waged as part of a long-term effort to bring more women and men into the suffrage camp.

Historians who have criticized AWSA's efforts as "exhausting labors" for "meager results" have failed to realize that these losing efforts were a necessary part of the long process of changing public opinion.[13] The reality is that the many ways in which AWSA and the *Woman's Journal* supported state suffrage movements between 1870 and 1890 laid the foundation for future successes.

At its inception, AWSA had grounds for optimism. The territories of Wyoming and Utah enfranchised women in 1869 and 1870, respectively. Though the seeds for woman suffrage blew in from the East, they first took root in the settler societies of the West. Several factors favored western progress, although each territory or state had its own unique sociopolitical constellation. Western areas were less bound by tradition, lacked established conservative institutions, respected the roles of pioneer women, and sought to attract more women settlers.

Additional successes were anticipated, particularly in the states of Michigan and Iowa, which had strong state suffrage associations. Speaking at AWSA's annual meeting in New York in May 1871, Stone stated, "The ideas which underlie the question of Woman Suffrage have reached the last stage of discussion before their final acceptance." After passing through periods of indifference, scorn, and moral agitation, these ideas have, she continued, "grown up…and now they are ushered into politics [where] politicians know perfectly well that our success is a foregone conclusion."[14]

But after Woodhull's radical declarations, optimism was replaced by apprehension. As progress stalled in both Iowa and Michigan, Stone remarked, "the heaviest millstone we carry is Free Love."[15] She sought to limit the damage Woodhull had caused by calling upon supporters to stress that AWSA was an ally—not an opponent—of the family. "We need every clean soul to help us," she wrote, "when such a flood of what is fatal to the peace and purity of the family is rolled in on our question."[16] Though NWSA supporters would later criticize what they called AWSA's "social conservatism," that emphasis on respectability helped the suffrage movement to outlast the Woodhull affair. Moreover, Stone was hardly conservative. When Massachusetts passed a revised law giving women additional rights to wages earned outside the family, for example, she acknowledged the progress made, but complained, "All that a wife earns (through domestic labor) in her family still counts for nothing."[17]

In an effort to focus public attention on the suffrage movement's connection to American political traditions, Stone capitalized on the centennial of the Boston Tea Party. On December 15, 1873, three thousand people gathered in Boston's Faneuil Hall to hear her insist that the U.S. government honor the slogan of "no taxation without representation" that had launched the American Revolution. She noted that many single and widowed women paid hefty taxes despite having no voice in government.

Abby Kelley Foster joined her in this campaign for good reason. In 1872, she and her husband had refused to pay taxes. The City of Worcester took possession of their home, but the Fosters refused to move. Stone's campaign made headlines across the country when two elderly single sisters in Connecticut, Abby and Julia Smith, refused to pay taxes, and the Town of Glastonbury seized their cows and land. Their plight engendered

Lucy Stone. *Courtesy of the Library of Congress.*

widespread sympathy, and the *Woman's Journal* reprinted many articles from other newspapers "highly encouraging to friends of Woman Suffrage."[18] It also published regular updates of the sisters' protracted but ultimately successful legal battle.

Throughout the 1870s and 1880s, AWSA relied on the grassroots model that had proved successful during the antislavery movement. Field agents and lecturers were deployed to make speeches, help organize state and local suffrage associations, and support state suffrage campaigns. Stone and her husband traveled as much as they could, given their obligations to the *Woman's Journal* and to their daughter, Alice. Consistent with its broad outreach, AWSA held conventions in different cities, including Philadelphia, St. Louis, New York, Michigan, Cincinnati, Indianapolis, and Omaha.

Margaret W. Campbell was a leading organizer and lecturer, as well as a close friend of Lucy Stone's, and a brief review of some of Campbell's work conveys the scope of AWSA's efforts.[19] Born in Maine in 1827, she later moved to Springfield, Massachusetts. She became a suffrage supporter when she read about the 1850 Worcester Convention. After supporting soldiers' aid societies during the Civil War, she turned her attention to enfranchising women.

Campbell began by organizing local suffrage societies in Berkshire, Hampden, Worcester, Plymouth and Essex Counties, Massachusetts. She then spent much of 1872 in Maine, where she organized the inaugural meeting of the Maine Woman Suffrage Association. She followed that with two years of organizing in Michigan, Illinois, Indiana, Iowa, Nebraska, and Colorado. Her husband, a painter, often accompanied her and sold portraits along the way to finance their travels.

During her stays in Michigan and Colorado, Campbell worked on AWSA's hard-fought campaigns in the two states. The Michigan state legislature agreed to place a woman suffrage amendment on the ballot in November 1874. The Michigan State Suffrage Association vowed to organize and canvass the entire state with help from Campbell and other eminent lecturers from the East. Despite the supporters' best efforts, the male voters soundly defeated the referendum, 136,000 to 40,000.

AWSA next targeted Colorado. As the territory prepared to be admitted as a state in 1876, AWSA hoped to persuade the constitutional convention to enfranchise women. Campbell spent the bulk of 1875 and 1876 engaged in this campaign. Her "lecture halls" included a small schoolhouse filled with miners "who had had too much to drink," the steps of a "roughly built hotel" and various riverbanks. She sometimes traveled on the back of a "sure-footed little burro" on terrain where "one misstep might plunge both animal and rider thousands of feet."

In the end, the Colorado constitutional convention did not enfranchise women. Convention delegates agreed, however, to hold a referendum in 1877 on the issue. Campbell returned to Colorado for this campaign. But despite the suffragists' best efforts, the referendum was defeated by a nearly two-to-one margin. Campbell returned east to work in New England before turning her focus to Iowa, Indiana, and Nebraska.

Following the defeats in Michigan and Colorado, AWSA adapted its strategy to make partial suffrage campaigns a mainstay of its repertory. Partial suffrage laws, such as those that would permit women to vote in municipal or presidential elections, required only majority approval of a state's legislators. In contrast, amendments to a state's constitution typically required legislative assent followed by approval of the all-male electorate. AWSA hoped that partial suffrage would serve as an entering wedge to normalize women voting, after which full enfranchisement might be obtained.

As AWSA and its state affiliates waged campaigns, the *Woman's Journal* offered news and encouragement to women each week. In addition to providing a steady stream of arguments in favor of woman suffrage, articles discussed the creation of new associations, fundraising strategies, the progress of legislation, firsthand campaign accounts, and reports of national, state, and local conventions. Articles also gave extensive coverage to other aspects of women's lives and publicized their achievements in the United States and internationally. The *Woman's Journal*'s optimistic tone in the face of defeats conveyed a firm belief in the inevitability of progress. On January 1, 1876, for example, in a New Year's message, Stone wrote that despite having thus far attained suffrage only in the Wyoming and Utah territories, women had made numerous other advances. They had entered the professions, more schools were admitting women, many states had new laws to protect married women, and public sentiment was more "humane and liberal." Women, she advised, should enter the nation's centennial year "with confident anticipation that the enfranchisement of Woman cannot long be postponed."[20]

The extraordinary scope of the *Woman's Journal* may be best conveyed by considering the diverse content of several issues. The October 1, 1870 issue, which ushered in the paper's tenth month, included articles on women voting in Wyoming, women's progress in Scotland and Prussia, the death of a pioneering woman lawyer, several state and local woman suffrage conventions, plus a picnic held by advocates for dress reform. Five years later, its issue of October 2, 1875, in addition to numerous suffrage updates, contained articles that critiqued "probate confiscation" in California, defended women who chose to remain single, and profiled a woman who had secretly worked (because her husband objected) and whose earnings saved the family from financial ruin.

Topics addressed on October 2, 1880, included school committee suffrage, women's work in the social sciences, the critical work of teachers (most of whom by then were women), an upcoming celebration in Worcester of the thirtieth anniversary of the First National Woman's Rights Convention of 1850, and a New York women's botanical study club. State updates from Maine, Kansas, Ohio, Michigan, and Indiana were included in the October 3, 1885 issue, along with a list of recent patents awarded to women inventors, updates from France and England, and Emma Lazarus's poem "The Bartholdi Statue" (better known as "The New Colossus"), which was later engraved on the plaque at the Bartholdi-designed Statue of Liberty. Each issue also shared personal updates about key players and included poems, humor, and ads.

In addition to her editorial work, Stone also labored to raise money and obtain ads for the newspaper. In 1877, she described one hard day to Margaret Campbell: "I walked miles to picture stores, crockery stores, grocery stores, book stores, to soap stores, to 'special sales' going up flight after flight of stairs…and for all my day's toil, I did not get a cent." Revealing the toll of her work, she continued, "And when I came home at night to find the house cold, the fire nearly out…it seemed as though the tired of a whole life came into my essence."[21] Ten years later, she might have been describing herself when she praised the contributions of the many older women who had by then labored for decades in the movement but "whose hearts have not grown old with the years, and whose interest in the great questions vital to humanity is as fresh as ever!"[22]

Stone also extended the reach of the *Woman's Journal* beyond its several thousand paid subscribers. Beginning in 1871, it produced leaflets containing

Women voting in Wyoming. *Frank Leslie's Illustrated Newspaper*, November 24, 1888. *Courtesy of the Library of Congress.*

arguments in support of woman suffrage. These were provided to state and local organizations for distribution to legislators, local newspapers, and others. New titles were announced nearly every year. By 1886, twenty-seven different leaflets had been introduced, and two years later, the figure had risen to thirty-six.[23] Stone and her husband also wrote to other newspapers urging them to reprint *Woman's Journal* articles at no charge.

Their daughter, Alice Stone Blackwell, began a long career as editor (she would later succeed her parents as editor-in-chief) of the *Woman's Journal* following her 1881 graduation from Boston University. In college, she had been elected president of her class, which consisted of twenty-six men and two women.[24] Beginning in 1887, she also created and edited a several-page weekly called the *Woman's Column*, which was offered to over one thousand newspapers for reprinting. Her arrival on the scene permitted her parents to engage in more travel. For example, they spent a month campaigning in Nebraska in 1882 during an unsuccessful attempt to enfranchise women. Stone Blackwell was a private person, and it's difficult to get a clear sense of her personality. Friends described her as shy but determined and independent-minded.

Despite AWSA's best efforts, by the end of the 1880s, women had gained full enfranchisement only in Washington territory (1883) and municipal suffrage in Kansas (1887). (The victory in Washington was fleeting; the territorial supreme court invalidated the suffrage law in 1887.) Women retained the vote in Wyoming territory. They had lost the vote in Utah territory, however. Congress revoked woman suffrage there as part of an anti-polygamy effort directed at Utah's Mormons.

Winning woman suffrage had proved far more difficult than advocates had imagined at the end of the Civil War. This was also true in AWSA's home state of Massachusetts, where woman suffrage confronted numerous challenges brought about by industrialization and its associated consequences. Because it emblemizes the campaigns fought in many northeastern states, the Massachusetts struggle is worth exploring in greater depth.

5
SETBACKS IN MASSACHUSETTS

When the American Woman Suffrage Association was formed in 1869, Lucy Stone intended the former abolitionist stronghold of Massachusetts to be a successful laboratory in which to demonstrate the wisdom of AWSA's state-based strategy. A state constitutional amendment enfranchising women would require the approval of the state House and Senate in two consecutive years, followed by ratification by a majority of the all-male voters. Stone and her allies believed that the Republican-dominated state legislature, which still included many former allies from the antislavery struggle, would readily give their support.

"Woman suffrage is a Republican issue in Massachusetts," declared the *Woman's Journal.*[1] Suffrage leaders did not, however, anticipate the many social and political changes that would transform Massachusetts in the years after the Civil War. These included a new conservative strain in the Republican Party, the growing strength of the Democratic Party due to the large number of Irish immigrants and the growth in the industrial working class, a new postwar temperance movement, and the emergence of a woman-led anti-suffrage movement. Each of these developments would pose new obstacles to the state's suffrage movement.

In January 1870, two months after AWSA held its inaugural convention in Cleveland, Stone and Julia Ward Howe headed the list of former Bay State abolitionists who announced a meeting for the purpose of organizing a state woman suffrage association.[2] The mission of the new Massachusetts Woman Suffrage Association (MWSA) was to spawn and support local associations that would campaign for a state constitutional amendment. Howe became president, and Stone served on the executive committee and led the finance committee. Other MWSA leaders included Mary Livermore and William Lloyd Garrison. Reflecting the close ties among MWSA, AWSA and the *Woman's Journal*, they all shared office space, briefly on Tremont Street and then on Park Street. (The New England Woman Suffrage Association also shared this space, but that association became less important after the state association formed.)

Many former abolitionists also joined the New England Woman's Club, which Julia Ward Howe and several others founded in 1869. The women's club movement began after the Civil War when women who had participated in war relief efforts wished to continue to meet and collaborate. The New England Women's Club provided a respectable meeting place where middle- and upper-class women could find camaraderie and pursue cultural and philanthropic activities. The club movement would come to play an important role in the suffrage tale.

Reflecting their founders' abolitionist roots, MWSA and the New England Women's Club, like AWSA, admitted black women.[3] In 1870, the African American population of Massachusetts was small, amounting to less than 2 percent of the state's 1.5 million residents. The state's black suffragists typically had a past connection to the abolitionist movement. Caroline Remond Putnam, who joined MWSA, was from Salem's best-known black family. Her brother and sister, Charles and Sarah Remond, had been leading abolitionist lecturers, and Putnam operated a women's hair salon and wig factory in Salem.[4]

Josephine St. Pierre Ruffin joined both MWSA and the New England Women's Club. She was born in Boston in 1842; her black father was the son of immigrants from Martinique, and her white mother hailed from England. At sixteen, she married George Ruffin, and they actively worked in the antislavery effort. In 1869, her husband became the first black graduate of Harvard Law School, and he would later become the state's first black judge. Years later, Ruffin wrote that she was welcomed into MWSA by Lucy Stone, Julia Ward Howe, and other "pioneer workers who were broad enough to include 'no distinction because of race' with 'no distinction because of sex.'"[5]

Even before MWSA was established, Stone had begun efforts to amend the Massachusetts Constitution. She helped convince the state legislature to create a joint special committee on woman suffrage and, in March 1869, she testified before it in support of an amendment that would remove the word *male* from the voter qualifications provision. Eight thousand women had signed pro-suffrage petitions. But foreshadowing future struggles with women who opposed the expansion of their own rights, nearly two hundred women from the town of Lancaster signed an anti-suffrage petition. They contended that gaining the vote would decrease the moral influence of women and "bring into the family circle a dangerous element of discord."[6] The joint special committee endorsed the woman suffrage amendment, but it was defeated in the legislature.

Once the battles over the Fourteenth and Fifteenth Amendments were concluded, suffragists anticipated that victory in Massachusetts was just around the corner. Stone and Mary Livermore addressed the Republican state convention in 1870. When the Victoria Woodhull scandal threatened to interrupt progress, MWSA hired several agents to hold dozens of meetings to rally supporters.

To suffragists' dismay, in 1872, the state legislature defeated a bill that would have recommended a constitutional amendment enfranchising women. Half the Republicans and nearly all the Democrats opposed the measure.[7] This vote laid bare the shifting social forces that would shape the struggle ahead.

After the Civil War, a substantial segment of the state Republican Party, like the national party, oriented itself away from social reform. A new breed of Gilded Age Republicans—industrialists and bankers, but also farmers and small businessmen—favored economic growth and believed in Social Darwinism. Most of these men thought women belonged in their traditional sphere. Ominously, even some who were more open-minded about gender relations did not want to disrupt the status quo at a time when immigration, industrialization, and labor unions were rapidly transforming the state.

Massachusetts suffragists had far less support in the minority Democratic Party, in which Catholic immigrants from Ireland formed a core constituency.[8] Many Irish Catholics still regarded woman suffragists and their Republican supporters as irredeemably tainted by the pre–Civil War association between abolitionists and nativists. That's because the Republican Party included remnants of the 1850s nativist Know Nothing Party. Additionally, Irish immigrants bore values crafted in a world dominated by tradition and patriarchy.

Though the state's politics would remain dominated by Republicans for several decades, continuing immigration would swell the number of Democrats, especially in urban areas. The City of Lawrence elected a Democratic mayor in 1881, and Boston did so in 1884. Massachusetts sent its first post–Civil War Democratic representative to Congress in 1876. Women trying to achieve suffrage in Massachusetts would need a strategy to capture significant Democratic support. But in the 1870s, no such strategy existed.

They did make one strategic change, however. MWSA, in parallel with AWSA, came out in support of a partial suffrage–first strategy. MWSA declared that it would seek suffrage in city and town elections and then renew the campaign for a state constitutional amendment.[9] In addition to requiring only legislative approval, municipal suffrage was less radical than full suffrage. Many municipal issues were, arguably, within a woman's traditional family-oriented sphere. After all, cities and towns were responsible for providing families with such amenities as clean water and safe streets and parks.

Here, they faced, however, another looming hurdle. Local governments also regulated the granting of liquor licenses. This nexus would lead to new alliances and animosities with lasting repercussions. Like the antislavery movement, the temperance movement had begun in the first, reformist decades of the nineteenth century, and Stone, Anthony, and Stanton were among the women's rights activists who had supported it. The temperance movement sought to shield women and children from the devastating consequences of excessive male drinking, including domestic violence, poverty, and abandonment.

A vigorous new anti-alcohol movement arose after the Civil War. A political party, the Prohibition Party, was founded in 1869, and the Woman's Christian Temperance Union (WCTU) was founded in Ohio in 1874. Two years later, MWSA, angry with Republican state legislators for not enfranchising women, endorsed the state's Prohibition Party, which supported woman suffrage.[10] But the Prohibition Party did poorly on election day. Afterward, regretting that the suffrage movement had angered Republican supporters, the *Woman's Journal* urged suffragists to avoid alliances with third parties and work only with the two major parties. AWSA subsequently followed suit and adopted a formal policy of party neutrality; it pledged "to use every honorable effort to secure the election of suffragists as legislators irrespective of party lines."[11]

Frances Willard. *Courtesy of the Library of Congress.*

An association between the WCTU and the woman suffrage movement would prove longer lasting. A formal link was forged when Frances Willard became a leader of the WCTU. Speaking in Boston in 1876, she announced that loving wives, daughters, sisters, and mothers should seek the ballot to protect their homes and the men they loved from the temptations of alcohol. In 1879, upon Willard's ascension to the organization's presidency, delegates approved a resolution supporting what she called the "Home Protection Ballot." Mary Livermore, who had been active in the prewar temperance movement, reinforced the bond between Massachusetts' temperance and suffrage movements when she led the state chapter of the WCTU from 1875 to 1885. In 1881, the WCTU endorsed municipal suffrage "by a very nearly unanimous vote."[12]

But the alliance with the temperance movement came at a significant cost. The WCTU was deeply Protestant, and a substantial number of its members blamed an alleged link between "Romanism and rum" for the impoverished state of Irish Catholic immigrants. This reinforced Catholics' distrust of the suffrage movement. Further, thousands who made their living as brewers, distillers, distributors, and saloon keepers saw women voters as a dangerous threat and pledged to oppose municipal suffrage.[13]

SCHOOL COMMITTEE SUFFRAGE: THE "LESSER" ENTERING WEDGE

As the campaign for municipal suffrage unfolded, Bay State women did gain the right to vote in school committee elections. MWSA was not the driving force behind this partial enfranchisement, however. In fact, it initially disfavored a campaign for school suffrage, which allowed women to vote only on issues directly connected to their traditional role of overseeing their children's education. MWSA considered school committee suffrage vastly inferior to full municipal suffrage.

The school suffrage effort originated when several members of the Education Committee of the New England Women's Club sought to serve on the Boston School Committee. Their effort was precipitated by a desire to improve children's physical and mental health, expand the movement for kindergartens, and increase opportunities for girls. Although the

Massachusetts Constitution provided that only men could vote, it did not limit the gender of office holders.

Abigail Williams May, whose managerial skills had made her New England's leader of the Sanitary Commission during the Civil War, became the public face of the school suffrage effort. Born into a reformist family, she was the cousin of Samuel May, whose lecture on women's rights had so influenced Lucy Stone. May and three other Women's Club members ran for the Boston School Committee in December 1873. Remarkably, they were elected. Their success demonstrates that many men viewed women's involvement with schools as consistent with their role as nurturers of children. Many men who favored restricting alcohol also believed that women would support temperance education in the public schools. A majority of the Boston School Committee refused to seat the women, however. This turn of events led MWSA to wryly observe, "Barbarism dies hard, and nowhere harder than in the Athens of America."[14] The legislature intervened, believing that women were well suited to serve on school committees, and the women took their seats.

The tenure of these pioneers was short-lived. May was defeated in 1878, and at the end of that year, only one woman remained on the school committee. Well aware that women voters would likely have retained the women members, the New England Women's Club sprang into action. Members petitioned the legislature to permit women to vote in school committee elections. They pointed out that neighboring New Hampshire, as well as Michigan and Minnesota, had such laws.

Despite its earlier reluctance, MWSA decided to support school committee suffrage. Passage would signify, Lucy Stone remarked, "the first actual break in the double wall built by custom and laws to shut women away from their political rights."[15] In April 1879, the Massachusetts legislature, by wide margins, enacted a law permitting women to vote in school committee elections (although it burdened women voters with a disproportionately high poll tax). The *Woman's Journal* promptly urged women to register and vote. Author Louisa May Alcott, who was also related to Abigail Williams May, was among the first to do so. Voting in the town of Concord, she reported that "no bolt fell on our audacious heads; no earthquake shook the town."[16] Ironically, Lucy Stone was not permitted to vote. Boston officials denied her a ballot when she refused to register under her married name.

MWSA was optimistic that the legislature, now having supported one form of partial suffrage, would relax its resistance to municipal suffrage. Along with AWSA, MWSA stressed the particular fitness of women to improve the

"Women voting at the municipal election in Boston on December 11," *Harper's Weekly*, December 15, 1888. Women were actually voting in the school committee election. *Courtesy of the Library of Congress.*

FROM FORCE OF
HABIT SHE WILL
CLEAN THIS UP.

LOU ROGERS

"From force of habit she will clean this up." Lou Rogers, *Judge*, February 8, 1913. This cartoon reflects suffragists' "municipal housecleaning" campaign. *Courtesy of HathiTrust.*

"bad housekeeping" in cities. While suffragists would continue to argue that they were entitled to vote as a matter of natural right, they would thereafter also employ arguments based on social expediency.[17]

Apparent momentum in support of woman suffrage gave rise to an ominous counter-reaction. In 1882, a group of thirteen influential Boston-area women organized in opposition to municipal suffrage. These "remonstrants," as they were called, may have been prodded into action by state senator George Crocker, who was closely allied with both conservative business and liquor interests. The remonstrants, who included Senator Crocker's wife, were nearly all Boston Brahmins (the white Anglo-Saxon Protestant descendants of early settlers who were members of Boston's social, economic, and political elite). They, like their husbands, feared any changes to the existing social order that granted them positions of privilege. The remonstrants presented anti-suffrage petitions stating that politics was outside a woman's proper sphere and would lead to the neglect of children and household responsibilities. They also argued that a woman's ability to do good works in society required her moral authority to remain untainted by partisan interests.[18]

Remonstrants quickly gained influence, including within the New England Women's Club. (Women's clubs would become a suffrage battleground.) Kate Gannett Wells, a vice president of the club, testified against municipal suffrage legislation in January 1885. She explained that she performed this "unwomanly" task in order to save women "from further imposition of political duties which we are not prepared to fulfill." She also argued that the suggestion that women opposed to suffrage could simply refrain from voting was flawed, because "when [women] see some measure we deem unwise likely to succeed, then, to save our country or State, we must vote." Wells also made clear the prejudices of conservative elites who were unwilling to expand the franchise. Describing her charitable work with poor immigrant women, she shared that "many a one spoke of the time when she could vote as the only vengeance left her to exercise upon the wealthy classes."[19]

The following year, 140 prominent men, including the president of Harvard University, published a newspaper advertisement opposing woman suffrage. Although suffragists continued to petition for municipal suffrage, the Massachusetts legislature defeated each piece of legislation by large margins.[20]

In 1888, Massachusetts suffragists faced a new challenge. By this time, Catholics held half of the twenty-four seats on the Boston School Committee. Sectarian conflict ensued when a report emerged that during a history lesson on the Middle Ages, a Protestant teacher had mocked the Catholic Church's attitude toward indulgences. When Catholics had the teacher censured, Protestants launched a campaign to defeat all Catholic school board candidates. Eleven of twenty-four seats were slated to be filled at the next election.[21]

The Republican Party put forth a slate of anti-Catholic candidates endorsed by a nativist women's group called the Loyal Women of America and by the Massachusetts chapter of the WCTU. The Democrats offered their own list of pro-Catholic candidates. Ednah Cheney, a leader in the drive for school committee enfranchisement, proposed a less divisive approach. A founder of the Massachusetts School Suffrage Association, she persuaded many fellow members to offer a slate of candidates opposed to sectarianism in the public schools.

As the election approached, the number of Protestant and Catholic women registered to vote grew from 3,200 to 25,000. Despite the opposition of the Catholic clergy, many Democratic politicians encouraged Catholic women to register and support the Democratic slate.

Although pleased to see the growth in voter registration, Lucy Stone and her daughter, Alice Stone Blackwell, were alarmed by the sectarian appeals. The *Woman's Journal* argued in favor of electing a school committee of "public-spirited men and women who know that the schools need to be

Alice Stone Blackwell. *Courtesy of the Library of Congress.*

useful and acceptable to all classes, creeds, and races, so as to educate the children of our various nationalities into enlightened American citizens."

On Election Day, the majority of voters elected the Republican slate endorsed by the Loyal Women of America. The election reinforced the belief of many Democrats that woman suffrage in Massachusetts was a Republican cause. Catholic clergy in the state renewed their contention that voting interfered with the domestic duties of Catholic women. *The Pilot*, the leading newspaper of Boston's Catholic community, opined that the Republican Party was the party of "intolerance and injustice," and any Democrat who supported woman suffrage was either a knave or a fool.[22]

THE "SHAM" SUFFRAGE REFERENDUM OF 1895

By the end of the 1880s, increasing numbers of Massachusetts Republicans supported municipal suffrage for women. Many nativist Republicans believed that the votes of Protestant woman (who were expected to vote in large numbers) would save the state from "rum and Romanism." Many reformist Republicans had been convinced that women's housekeeping skills would address the many challenges posed by urbanization, industrialization, and immigration. Some Republicans continued to believe that suffrage was a natural right of citizens.

The state's Republican Party remained deeply divided on this issue, however. The committee of remonstrants reacted to increased prospects for municipal suffrage by beginning an annual newsletter, the *Remonstrance*, in 1890, which was edited anonymously by journalist Frank Foxcroft. The *Remonstrance* asserted that the "great majority" of women did not want the ballot, and to "force" it upon them would be an injustice and "lessen their influence for good and imperil the community."[23] With the inception of the *Remonstrance*, Massachusetts became the center of the emerging women's anti-suffrage movement.

The rapid growth of industrialization raised a challenge from another quarter. The 1880s and 1890s were a time of labor conflict that pitted management against newly unionized laborers. Republicans with business interests feared that women voters would support legislators who favored laws beneficial to laborers, especially women and children working in factories.

Additionally, Boston was a center of a new wave of anti-immigration sentiment that swept through conservative Republican circles. These conservatives believed in governance by the elite and opposed any expansion of the franchise, particularly to uneducated immigrants from eastern and southern Europe. In 1892, the state legislature enacted a statute providing that a voter must be able to write his name and read at least three lines of the state constitution.[24]

Nevertheless, Republican support for municipal suffrage continued to increase. In March 1893, the Massachusetts House narrowly defeated municipal suffrage 102–111; 94 Republicans and 8 Democrats voted in favor, while 45 Republicans and 66 Democrats were opposed. The state senate did not vote on municipal suffrage legislation that year.[25]

The women's movement also suffered a grave personal loss that year. On October 18, 1893, seventy-five-year-old Lucy Stone died from stomach cancer. Her daughter, Alice Stone Blackwell, reported her mother's last words of advice: "Make the world better." The next issue of the *Woman's Journal* included numerous tributes to the iconic figure. Her daughter's summary of her mother's life pointedly noted that she "always craved, not the post of prominence, but the post of work."[26] From this time onward, Stone Blackwell's independent streak emerged; she began to pursue numerous humanitarian causes, such as assisting Armenian refugees, in addition to her continued work for woman suffrage.

At the twenty-fifth annual meeting of MWSA, held two months after her mother's death, Alice Stone Blackwell announced a comprehensive blueprint to win municipal suffrage. Plans included the establishment of additional local leagues, press outreach, pro-suffrage essay contests, and suffrage booths at county fairs. This renewed effort had partial success. In 1894, the Massachusetts House supported municipal suffrage, 118–107; the Senate defeated it, 14–24. Victory appeared tantalizingly close.[27]

Anti-suffragists mobilized in response to the close vote. They argued suffrage should not be "thrust" upon women without proof that the majority of them wished to vote. Opponents persuaded legislators to schedule a nonbinding "informational" referendum on November 2, 1895. Men voting in the state election and women voting in the school committee election would receive a separate ballot containing one question: "Is it expedient that municipal suffrage should be extended to women?"[28]

Suffrage supporters were furious at what they called the "sham referendum." MWSA initially intended to recommend a boycott but then changed course. Alice Stone Blackwell explained that suffragists decided to "stir up as much agitation and discussion of the question as possible and to use it as a means of education."[29]

Some suffrage backers used the pending referendum to make divisive partisan appeals, however. The Loyal Women of America forecast that women voters would save the state from Romanism. Temperance advocates predicted that women voters would enact alcohol restrictions. Henry Blackwell suggested many reasons to support municipal suffrage, including appeals to justice and what he called women's superior morality. But he also appealed to anti-immigrant Republicans when he observed that, due to native-born women's greater desire to participate and the state's literacy law, enfranchising women would add many more native-born voters than foreign-born ones.[30]

The remonstrants, meanwhile, shaped a strategy that would permit them to use the referendum to full advantage. Organizing as the Massachusetts Association Opposed to the Further Extension of Suffrage to Women, they urged women not to vote. They maintained that every woman who abstained from voting was, in effect, voting "no." After all, they claimed, women opposed to voting could not reasonably be expected to go to the polls to show their opposition.[31]

The remonstrants' efforts were supported, both financially and organizationally, by the Man Suffrage Association, which was formed to defeat the referendum. Francis C. Lowell, a Boston Brahmin and Harvard trustee whose wife was a remonstrant, chaired the Man Suffrage Association. Members included wealthy and influential businessmen, lawyers, and academics. Reflecting the wealth of its members—and the power of money in politics—the Man Suffrage Association spent $3,600 to defeat the referendum, while pro-suffrage forces raised only $1,300. The Man Suffrage Association "covered walls and fences from one end of the state to the other with huge placards" urging opposition.[32]

Democrats also mounted extensive opposition to the referendum. Many in the Irish Catholic wing of the party continued to associate woman suffrage with nativism, temperance, and anti-family radicalism. Although some Democratic labor leaders believed that women voters would help elect pro-labor candidates, the state's still young labor movement largely remained on the sidelines during the referendum campaign. When Henry Blackwell asked the 150 labor organizations in the state how they felt, only 34 unions replied in favor of suffrage; 5 were opposed, and 111 ignored the inquiry.[33]

On Election Day, male voters decisively defeated the referendum: 87,000 men agreed it would be "expedient" to extend municipal suffrage to women, but 187,000 disagreed. The 4 percent of women who voted overwhelmingly supported expanding suffrage: 22,204–864. The *Remonstrance*, offering its own interpretation of the women's vote, gleefully reported that 96 percent of women were opposed or indifferent to suffrage.[34]

Led by the *Woman's Journal*, the suffragists tried to put a positive spin on the disastrous outcome, noting that one-third of men and 96 percent of women who voted favored expanding suffrage. Alice Stone Blackwell maintained that suffrage was inevitable and that the presumed indifference of many women was inconsequential. Why, she wrote, should those who do not care to vote prevent those who *do* care from voting? She also noted that the referendum had stirred up an unprecedented amount of interest in the subject. Her less diplomatic father wrote that a geographical analysis of election results showed that "intelligent, active, wide-minded" middle-class men favored woman suffrage. He identified opponents as immigrants with "old world prejudices," representatives of "the liquor traffic [and] the monopolies," and those blinded by the "exclusiveness of wealth" and the "bigotry of tradition."[35]

Despite attempts to look for a silver lining, the referendum was experienced as an enormous defeat by the suffrage movement, and the consequences were quickly felt. Many local chapters of MWSA shrank in size or disbanded, and remaining members were often middle-aged or elderly.[36] The Massachusetts defeat also cast a long shadow over the entire nation's suffrage movement. Opponents claimed they now had irrefutable evidence that women did not wish to vote, and that the subject should not again be raised until such time as women clearly demonstrated that desire.[37]

The National American Woman Suffrage Association

During the late 1880s, Alice Stone Blackwell's focus on the suffrage campaign had expanded beyond the Massachusetts campaigns and the *Woman's Journal*. A primary accomplishment was her leading role in the negotiations that led to the union of AWSA and NWSA into the new National American Woman Suffrage Association (NAWSA) in 1890. Her mother and other members of the first generation of suffragists were aging. This, coupled with the discouraging state of the movement, led members of the next generation to take up the charge.

The enthusiasm for uniting the two suffrage associations came about after a number of defeats. Eight years before the Massachusetts loss in 1895, the U.S. Senate had voted for the first and only time in the nineteenth century on an amendment that read, "The right of citizens in the United States to vote shall not be denied or abridged by the United States or by any State on account of sex." (The House would not vote for the first time until 1915.) Senator Henry Blair, a pro-suffrage Republican from New Hampshire, succeeded in bringing the measure to the floor. Massachusetts senator George Frisbie Hoar, one of the remaining Republicans with roots in the abolitionist era, was among those who spoke in support. When the Senate voted on January 25, 1887, though, only sixteen senators (fifteen of them Republicans) supported the measure, while thirty-four were opposed. Twenty-six senators were absent, including Massachusetts' other senator, Republican Henry Dawes.[1] Congress delivered another defeat that year. It passed an anti-polygamy law, directed at Utah's Mormons, which included a provision revoking woman suffrage in the Utah territory.

The movement had additionally suffered recent setbacks within the states. Also in 1887, male voters in Rhode Island became the first in the East to vote on a proposed woman suffrage amendment to a state constitution. They overwhelmingly defeated the measure twenty-two thousand to seven thousand.[2] Across the country, the Washington Territorial Supreme Court rescinded the legislature's enfranchisement of women, concluding that the territorial law conflicted with federal law.

Still, there were some rays of sunshine in western states. Women continued to vote in the territory of Wyoming, and when it was admitted to statehood in 1890, women were fully enfranchised in one state. Several years earlier, in 1887, Kansas had enacted a law permitting women to vote in municipal elections. During that campaign, suffragists wore yellow ribbons to represent the Kansas sunflower. They chose it because "as the sunflower follows civilization, follows the wheel track and the plow, so woman suffrage inevitably follows civilized government."[3] Suffragists in other states followed suit, and the yellow sunflower became a symbol of the movement.

Younger members frustrated by the slow progress of suffrage were also perplexed by the existence of two rival suffrage organizations with overlapping missions and methods. Wouldn't, they wondered, one unified organization have more clout? Though precise membership numbers don't exist, AWSA and NWSA had fewer than 10,000 dues-paying members between them.[4] Meanwhile, women had demonstrated in far larger numbers their willingness to join other organizations. The Woman's Christian Temperance Union had nearly 200,000 members.[5] There had been explosive growth in the number of women's clubs.

In the late 1880s, several leaders of the next generation, including Alice Stone Blackwell and NWSA's Rachel Foster, decided that AWSA and NWSA must put aside old grievances and join forces. The three aging leaders of the suffrage movement understood the potential benefits of the merger and agreed to allow Stone Blackwell and Foster to lead negotiations.

Negotiating unification had many tense moments. Some involved Anthony's and Stanton's continued insistence that the Seneca Falls Convention gave birth to the woman suffrage movement. The acrimony engendered by this subject was very fresh. In 1888, Lucy Stone had agreed to speak at the first gathering of the International Council of Women, an organization formed by Anthony and Stanton to foster global connections among women's rights activists. The two scheduled the founding convention to coincide with the fortieth anniversary of the Seneca Falls Convention, which they persisted in calling the first public demand for women's rights. Incensed, Stone wrote to her sister-in-law, Antoinette Brown Blackwell, "I think we ought to puncture the bubble that the Seneca Falls meeting was the first public demand for suffrage."[6]

In her public remarks, Stone did her best to flesh out the story of the movement's origins. She credited abolitionists Angelina and Sarah Grimké and Abby Kelley Foster with starting the women's rights movement when they spoke

An older Lucy Stone. *Courtesy of the Library of Congress.*

out against slavery and "[a]ll the cyclones and blizzards which prejudice, bigotry and custom could raise were let loose upon these three peerless women." Stone emphasized her own "solitary battle for woman's rights," which began in 1847. Pointedly, she added that news of the Seneca Falls Convention did not reach her as she "went from city to city and State to State, carrying the good gospel of equal rights, and seeking to create that wholesome discontent among women, which would make them resent their unequal condition and wish to escape from it." She stressed the significance of the Worcester Convention of 1850.[7] But Stone's efforts were Sisyphean. By this time, historical memory had absorbed the legend of Seneca Falls and would perpetuate it. Stone and other AWSA founders had been reclassified as "supporting cast members."[8]

Despite tensions, the negotiations eventually succeeded, and the National American Woman Suffrage Association (NAWSA) was born in 1890. Stone, who had a respiratory illness, was unable to attend the founding convention. She had futilely sought an agreement that NAWSA would not be led by herself, Anthony, or Stanton. The convention elected Stanton president, Anthony vice-president, and the absent Stone chair of the executive committee. Seventy-year-old Anthony, however, led NAWSA from the outset. Stanton departed for a lengthy visit to England, where her daughter, Harriot, lived, and resigned as president two years later. Stone, who viewed her selection as "complimentary," chose to focus her energy on the *Woman's*

An older Susan B. Anthony (*standing*) and Elizabeth Cady Stanton. *Courtesy of the Library of Congress.*

Journal until her death three years later.[9] Anthony largely ran NAWSA out of Rochester, New York, in the home she shared with her sister, Mary.

Although the creation of NAWSA meant that Massachusetts lost its status as the home of a national suffrage organization, the *Woman's Journal* continued to be based in Boston and remained the recognized mouthpiece of the movement. Further cementing the ties between NAWSA and the *Woman's Journal*, Stone Blackwell became NAWSA's corresponding secretary. As discussed in subsequent chapters, Massachusetts continued to produce national leaders and pilot innovations that would be replicated elsewhere.

Moreover, validating the success of AWSA's state-based approach, NAWSA was the strategic successor to AWSA despite being led by Anthony. The new organization continued AWSA's concentration on state campaigns, budgeting zero funds for lobbying Congress. Annual conventions alternated between Washington, D.C., and other cities. NAWSA additionally adopted AWSA's single-minded focus on suffrage. NAWSA was also firmly nonpartisan: it was committed to the election of suffrage supporters regardless of political party. Structurally, NAWSA adopted AWSA's representative structure; state societies selected delegates who became voting members of NAWSA.

But NAWSA carried on one significant and unfortunate NWSA tradition. Stone and AWSA's other abolitionist founders had protested both race- and gender-based discrimination. When NAWSA was formed, Julia Ward Howe expressed her concern that the new organization would abandon AWSA's commitment to racial equality.[10] Her worry was well founded. NAWSA fully decoupled woman suffrage from black suffrage.

As with the other social currents swirling during this time period, historical timing played a role in this decision. NAWSA was created during the Jim Crow era, when southern states passed laws to enforce segregation and undercut the protections of the Fourteenth and Fifteenth Amendments. New voting laws effectively disenfranchised black men through devices such as poll taxes, literacy tests, and grandfather clauses. White supremacists used lynching and other forms of terror to subjugate blacks. White northerners remained largely silent, as reconciliation between whites in the North and the South was another hallmark of the Jim Crow era.

NAWSA reinvigorated the racist doctrine of "educated suffrage": the argument that better-educated women were more worthy of the vote than uneducated black and immigrant men and that women voters would raise the intellectual and moral quality of the electorate. While in part a strategic decision intended to curry support from white southerners, the position also reflected the genuine convictions of many in NAWSA. Elizabeth Cady Stanton reiterated her support for educated suffrage, writing that to protect the nation from the "ignorant and impecunious from the Old World landing on our shores by hundreds every day, we must have some restrictions of the suffrage."[11] Henry Blackwell did not advocate rolling back male suffrage. But he pointed out that the votes of educated women could counter the votes of "two great bodies of illiterate citizens; in the North, people of foreign birth; in the South, people of African race."[12] (He assumed that educated women were more likely to vote than uneducated ones; moreover, many states imposed their own literacy requirements on voters.)

Some raised their voices in opposition. In an essay published in the *Woman's Journal*, Harriot Stanton Blatch (Elizabeth Cady Stanton's daughter) asserted that literacy was not necessarily correlated with morality or sound judgment.[13] Yet despite isolated protests, NAWSA in 1893 adopted a resolution calling "attention to the significant facts that in every State there are more [white] women who can read and write than all negro voters; more American women who can read and write than all foreign voters."[14]

Though the native-born Protestants who dominated NAWSA would eventually recognize the practical necessity of an alliance with white working-class women (many of whom were first- or second-generation Catholic or Jewish immigrants from Ireland, Italy, or Eastern Europe), discrimination against African Americans would stain the remainder of NAWSA's history. To allay concerns of white southerners, Anthony even asked Frederick Douglass not to attend the 1895 NAWSA convention in Atlanta, the first held south of the Mason-Dixon line.

That same year, NAWSA faced a divisive challenge of another sort. Stanton published her *Woman's Bible*, in which she challenged degrading portrayals of women in the Bible. Among other claims, she posited that the Christian Trinity was composed of a "Heavenly Mother, Father, and Son." Her heretical views threatened to undermine NAWSA's united focus on suffrage and invited accusations that suffragists were subversive radicals. A resolution was introduced at the January 1896 convention, which Stanton did not attend, disavowing any connection between NAWSA and the *Woman's Bible*. Stone Blackwell was among those who spoke in favor of the resolution. Despite Anthony's plea not to "censure" Stanton, the majority of delegates approved it.[15]

Stanton's *Bible* also offended Jewish suffragists, a small but growing group. Stanton blamed the "God of the Hebrews" for women's inferior status and denigrated Jews with a variety of negative stereotypes. Though many Jewish women ultimately supported the twentieth-century suffrage movement, mistrust lingered.

Meanwhile, during the 1890s, Anthony maintained a strenuous travel schedule as NAWSA supported pending state campaigns in an effort to generate momentum and attract favorable publicity. NAWSA celebrated in 1893 when Colorado enfranchised women and New Zealand became the first nation to do so. Anthony drew additional attention to women's rights that year when she addressed the World Congress of Representative Women at the Columbian Exposition in Chicago. In 1895, Utah was admitted to statehood, and the new state constitution enfranchised women. That same year, however, was when Massachusetts voters handed the suffrage movement a major defeat in the "sham referendum."

Both Idaho and California planned referenda on proposed state amendments to enfranchise women in November 1896. Idaho voted in favor, but the California referendum failed when 55 percent of male voters voted against it. The California defeat interrupted the run of recent gains in the West. The Massachusetts and California defeats, coupled with the divisions caused by Stanton's *Bible*, laid bare the need for the woman suffrage movement to reenergize and refocus for the new century.

New Leadership

Forty-one-year-old Carrie Chapman Catt succeeded eighty-year-old Anthony as NAWSA president in 1900. This changing of the guard would result in extraordinary gains. Catt, a brilliant tactician, remodeled NAWSA and positioned it for ultimate success. Under her leadership, state suffrage associations, including the Massachusetts Woman Suffrage Association, entered a period of experimentation and innovation. The result was stunning growth in the suffrage movement. NAWSA, which had 12,000 enrolled members in 1906, claimed over 117,000 members in 1910.[16]

Catt was born in Wisconsin, but she spent most of her childhood in Iowa. She attended Iowa State Agricultural College, where she was the only woman in her graduating class. She became a schoolteacher and then school superintendent in Mason City, Iowa, an unusual position for a woman of that era. Yet she joined the woman suffrage movement in a fashion that harkened back to the past. While attending Iowa's annual woman suffrage convention in 1885, she heard Lucy Stone speak. Roused by her call to action, Catt dedicated herself to obtaining the ballot for women.

In 1890, she married George Catt, an engineer who enthusiastically supported her involvement in woman suffrage activities. She became the leader of Iowa's suffrage association and attended national conventions. Rising quickly through NAWSA's ranks, she became chair of its National Organizing Committee in 1895. She was a leader of Colorado's successful 1893 campaign and spearheaded Idaho's successful 1896 campaign. She oversaw the establishment or revival of state and local suffrage organizations in many states. By 1899, every state had at least a "rudimentary" organization.[17] When Anthony selected Catt as her successor the following year, Stone Blackwell praised this as the "wisest possible choice."[18]

What personal qualities Catt possessed that inspired such confidence is less well known. As has been true with some of the other suffragists discussed, it is difficult to assess Catt's personality. Biographers have focused on her public life because she carefully concealed her private thoughts from public view.[19]

Catt understood that securing women's right to vote required changing public opinion. Many other gains in women's rights, including access to higher education and the professions, had required only small numbers of women committed to breaking barriers as well as some "broad and just-minded men." In these cases, Catt explained, the forces of ignorance, bigotry, conservatism, and fear were powerless to oppose change. Woman suffrage, in contrast, required the support of ordinary voters and could therefore not be achieved until popular opinion was prepared to grant it.[20] An exceptional strategist, Catt developed a multipronged plan to increase the visibility and mainstream appeal of the suffrage movement.

She set to work in a nation vastly different from the antebellum one in which the woman suffrage movement had begun. The suffrage movement so far had not adapted very well to the cataclysmic economic and social changes in the years since the Civil

Carrie Chapman Catt. *Courtesy of the Library of Congress.*

War that had transformed the United States into an industrial powerhouse. At the turn of the century, the public demanded solutions to the tremendous challenges posed by massive industrialization, immigration, urbanization, and government corruption. The Gilded Age, with its emphasis on Social Darwinism, gave way to the Progressive Era, which was characterized by a belief in the power of reform efforts to "clean up" both city life and government. Progressive reformers believed that restraining big business, exposing government corruption, and providing safe environments for people in urban neighborhoods and the workplace would improve society. Catt seized the opportunities created by new circumstances to forge a broader and more mainstream suffrage movement.

Creating a new, popular image of suffragists was a top priority. Catt sought to make clear that NAWSA was the ally, not the adversary, of modern but moderate women. For decades, the press had depicted suffragists as radical, masculine-looking, and humorless. Now, with the help of talented illustrators and cartoonists like Blanche Ames, Annie "Lou" Rogers and Nell Brinkley, the suffrage movement reinvented the popular image of the suffragist. To attract younger women, suffragists were portrayed as young, feminine, fashionable, and independent—but not radical or threatening. To attract married homemakers, suffragists were depicted as embracing motherhood. These cartoonists emphasized that suffrage opponents were the ones out of lockstep with mainstream American women. Boardman Robinson's illustration demonstrates the dramatic success of this campaign.

Even Susan B. Anthony was not spared a makeover. (Elizabeth Cady Stanton never regained favor after the *Woman's Bible* and had died in 1902.) NAWSA "repackaged" Anthony as a grandmotherly figure who enjoyed cooking, cleaning, and "teaching her nieces her wonderful method of darning rents in garments and household linens." NAWSA also stressed the extreme affection Anthony had for her youngest sister, Mary, whose "faithful and constant home-making" had allowed Anthony to dedicate herself to suffrage. Anthony additionally gave numerous copies of *History of Woman Suffrage* to NAWSA, which distributed it to libraries throughout the nation, and cooperated with Ida Husted Harper, who wrote a three-volume "authorized" biography. These acts contributed to her becoming a national icon. "Saint Susan" was venerated at annual NAWSA conventions, which were scheduled to coincide with her birthday.[21]

Catt initiated the "society plan" to recruit affluent socialites and influential club women to the movement, an effort that boosted both NAWSA's financial state and its public image. In an early effort, taking place during

THE TYPE HAS CHANGED.

"The Type Has Changed," Boardman Robinson, *New York Tribune*, February 24, 1911. This cartoon shows the success of NAWSA's campaign to improve the public image of suffragists. *Courtesy of the Library of Congress.*

the last year of Lucy Stone's life, the two had collaborated to recruit some of Denver's most elite women to support the successful Colorado campaign of 1893. The results had brought sorely needed funds and led to extensive, respectful press coverage. Catt initiated an effort to replicate this feat nationwide by having suffragists develop personal connections with wealthy women who might be sympathetic to the movement.[22]

As part of the effort to generate mainstream support, Catt avoided issues that might lead to dissent among suffragists or potential allies. Though she had once strongly supported temperance, she now distanced the suffrage movement from this divisive issue. NAWSA remained resolutely nonpartisan. She continued NAWSA's pursuit of support from white southerners. In a blatant acquiescence to Jim Crow racism, NAWSA announced in 1903 that its goal was to "do away with the requirement of a sex qualification for suffrage" and that "what other qualifications shall be asked for [suffrage] it leaves to each state."[23]

Catt also led the creation of a new international organization to press for woman suffrage. Active movements existed in many other nations, mostly in the British Commonwealth and Europe. She invited international representatives to attend the 1902 NAWSA convention in Washington, and delegates from eleven nations did so. They established the International Alliance of Woman Suffrage. The Alliance facilitated what would become critical connections between the American and British suffrage movements in the decades to come.

Catt stepped down as NAWSA head in 1904 to care for her ill husband, though she also admitted to the *Woman's Journal* that her exhausting schedule made a rest necessary.[24] After her husband's death the following year, she focused her efforts on leading the Alliance and on state campaigns, particularly in New York.

"Two Pedestals," Blanche Ames, *Boston Transcript*, 1915. Suffragists were determined to show that the vote was consistent with traditional values and that anti-suffrage sentiments were based on "sham chivalry." *Courtesy of the Sophia Smith Collection, Smith College.*

Reverend Anna Howard Shaw succeeded Catt. Shaw, who was then fifty-seven, had overcome an impoverished childhood in a desolate region of northern Michigan to become, in 1878, the second woman graduate of Boston University School of Theology. Her work with impoverished women and children in Boston's poorest neighborhoods led her to fight to improve their condition; she both obtained a medical degree from Boston University and joined the organized suffrage movement as a lecturer for MWSA. She served as NAWSA vice president from 1892 to 1904.

Stylistically, Shaw was a different sort of leader. While Catt was an organizational genius, Shaw's greatest strength was her exceptional oratory skills. When Susan B. Anthony died in March 1906, Shaw rallied suffragists not to despair that Anthony died before the struggle for suffrage had ended but to instead view her life "as a triumphal march, marked by sorrow and hardship, but never by despair." Shaw generally maintained Catt's policies, including NAWSA's acquiescence to racial discrimination. Shaw added an additional justification for racism; she claimed that black men were steadfast opponents of women suffrage. When some in NAWSA wanted to introduce a resolution opposing southern disenfranchisement of black men, she objected because "if our resolution were carried, [black men] would go straight to the polls and defeat us every time."[25] Black leader W.E.B. Du Bois accused her of a "barefaced falsehood."[26] A key exception to continuity with Catt's policies, however, was that Shaw maintained her longstanding ties to the temperance movement, which gave anti-prohibition forces reason to remain hostile to woman suffrage.

Shaw continued Catt's society plan. One notable recruit bears particular mention. In 1909, financial support from the fabulously wealthy Alva Smith (Vanderbilt) Belmont allowed NAWSA to afford a New York City headquarters and establish a national press department. Belmont had married William K. Vanderbilt, a grandson of shipping and railroad tycoon Cornelius Vanderbilt, in 1875. She became a fixture in society pages and built a lavish summer palace, Marble House, in Newport, Rhode Island. Rebuffing convention, she divorced her adulterous husband and married a wealthy investment banker, Oliver H.P. Belmont. After his death in 1908, she devoted her energy and fortune to woman suffrage.

During these years, NAWSA remained committed to its state-based strategy, still confident that a federal amendment would become feasible only after women were enfranchised in a critical number of states. Success would require, therefore, state associations also to change with the times. An in-depth look at Massachusetts illustrates how a cadre of energetic and creative women implemented change and propelled both the state and national movements forward.

7
NEW ALLIANCES

As the twentieth century dawned, inventive leaders in Massachusetts revitalized the state's suffrage movement by attracting new constituencies, forming new alliances, and experimenting with new tactics.[1] Exploring suffrage from the perspective of this one state reveals both the progress and challenges in the movement in a northeastern state that had rapidly urbanized and industrialized. Studying Massachusetts also advances our understanding of the national movement. As the *Woman's Journal* and NAWSA publicized and endorsed state innovations—and as leading suffragists continued to tirelessly crisscross the nation—NAWSA itself became larger, more diverse (albeit still white), and more influential.

A brief snapshot of Massachusetts at the turn of the century provides helpful context.[2] In 1870, the Bay State's population was almost 1.5 million. Thirty years later, the population had nearly doubled to 2.8 million. In 1900, more than half the state's population were immigrants or their children; in Boston, the figure approached 75 percent. The vast majority of immigrants arriving between 1840 and 1880 were Irish. Toward the end of the century, Italians and Eastern Europeans flocked to the state, where they clustered in urban ethnic enclaves. By 1900, roughly 4 percent of the state's population had been born in Italy and over 5 percent in Russia (of whom half were Jewish). During these years of explosive growth, the African American population of remained small, amounting to under 2 percent.

In the early twentieth century, Massachusetts was the most urban state in the nation; fully three-quarters of its residents lived in cities, and less than 10 percent of the state's labor force worked in agriculture. In addition to Boston, large industrial cities included Fall River, Lowell, Springfield, and Worcester. Three-quarters of factory workers were first- or second-generation Americans. Cities teemed with impoverished immigrants who lived in crowded tenements and worked under harsh conditions in factories that manufactured textiles, shoes, and other products. Others worked in construction and in quarries. Increasing numbers of workers unionized as they sought relief from low wages, long hours, and dangerous machines and conditions. When financial circumstances required, immigrant women and children labored in garment factories or laundries or worked in domestic service.

Life had also changed for white, native-born women of the working- and lower-middle classes who were no longer isolated on family farms. A complex urban economy—and inventions such as the typewriter, telephone, and department store—led to a demand for women to fill positions as typists, bookkeepers, telephone operators, and sales clerks. Women constituted 3.1 percent of clerical workers in 1870 but nearly 30 percent by 1900. By 1920, 92 percent of stenographers were female. Work for these women was largely a temporary endeavor, however, that ended with marriage. Nearly 90 percent of the female workforce were single, and another 4 percent were widows.

Young women from more privileged backgrounds also enjoyed new opportunities. In 1870, fewer than fourteen thousand American women had been enrolled in higher education; in 1900, that figure was over eighty-five thousand, which represented one-third of all students. Over half of these young women were enrolled in teacher-training schools. Teaching remained one of the few socially acceptable vocations for single middle-class women, and three-quarters of primary school teachers were women. Daughters of the upper class and the growing professional class might attend one of the Seven Sisters colleges, four of which (Mount Holyoke, Radcliffe, Smith and Wellesley) were located in Massachusetts, or a coeducational university such as Boston University, which opened in 1872. These colleges offered women the same liberal arts education available to men. Most women college graduates left the workforce after marriage (or married while in school and never entered the workforce), but some worked after marriage, some delayed marriage, and others remained single. Small numbers of women became doctors, journalists, ministers, or lawyers (the professional field most associated with public life).

Opportunities for independence and mobility opened up. The nationwide bicycle craze of the 1890s affected young women to such an extent that Anthony observed in 1896 that the bicycle was doing "more to emancipate women than anything else in the world."[3] Women who rode bicycles experienced the independence of transporting themselves and the energizing effects of exercise. The bicycle led to clothing reforms as young women spurned confining corsets and ballooning skirts. Streetlights, trolleys, subways, and elevated rails contributed to the ability of city-dwelling women to move about safely and independently.

Life also changed for economically secure married women. They had fewer children; the birthrate for white women fell from five in 1860 to three and a half in 1910. Economically advantaged women had access to inexpensive domestic help (provided by African American or immigrant women), store-bought goods, and new labor-saving home appliances. As a result, these women often had leisure hours to devote to women's clubs. While many club women focused on self-education and self-improvement, others looked outward for ways to provide the "municipal housekeeping" needed to clean up, or at least ameliorate, the harsh conditions caused by overcrowded cities and urban poverty. The Massachusetts Federation of Women's Clubs was founded in 1893, and by 1900, more than eight thousand Massachusetts women belonged to over fifty-five women's clubs.

Activists from Massachusetts took advantage of the new circumstances to found organizations that broadened and strengthened the woman suffrage movement across the social spectrum, attracting not only college students and alumnae but also working-class women. From these two prongs of development emerged important new leaders.

COLLEGE WOMEN

"I sat on the floor in [the headmistress's] little room and indignantly denied in my own mind all that she was saying, by way of advice to the seniors, about the duty of a wife to realize that the husband should be considered the head of the household....I was certain that she was wrong; for why should a woman be subordinate?"[4] This moment sparked Maud Wood Park's lifelong commitment to women's rights. The daughter of a Boston police officer, she attended boarding school in Albany, New York, graduating as class valedictorian in 1887. Following the same path as many earlier reformers, she taught school for eight years while saving money for college. Like her forebears, she had boundless energy. In a personal reflection composed in

1903, she wrote that she had "ambitions enough for Shakespeare and Julius Caesar and Cleopatra and Napoleon rolled into one."[5]

Park entered Radcliffe College in 1895, married architect Charles E. Park while a student, and graduated in three years. She voted in a school committee election before college but was "unaware or neglectful" of the Massachusetts 1895 municipal suffrage referendum. Perhaps motivated by that referendum, one of her English professors assigned students to write an essay on woman suffrage. Out of seventy students, Park was one of two who wrote in support. She declared, "I see no more reason for the men of my family to decide my political opinions and express them for me at the polls than to choose my hats and wear them, or my religious faith and occupy my seat in church." She found it "obvious" that one of two logical arguments should prevail. If women are the same as men for voting purposes, then women have the same need to vote as men. If women are different from men for voting purposes, then their different interests and points of view must be represented.[6]

But many college women in Massachusetts did not share Park's views. Agnes Irwin, the dean of Radcliffe from 1894 to 1909, was a prominent anti-suffragist (as was Harvard University president Charles Eliot). Mount Holyoke had conducted a straw poll at the time of the state's 1895 referendum; only 300 of 1,000 students participated, 114 of whom supported woman suffrage.[7]

After the Massachusetts Association Opposed to the Further Extension of Suffrage to Woman hosted an anti-suffrage speaker at Radcliffe, Park and a like-minded classmate, Inez Haynes, invited Alice Stone Blackwell to speak on campus.[8] This event, Park later recalled, "began the link that bound me to suffrage work for more than twenty years." Stone Blackwell invited Park to speak at MWSA's annual dinner and then before the Judiciary Committee of the Massachusetts Legislature. Her abilities impressed many veterans of the Massachusetts suffrage movement, including Mary Hutcheson Page, who had an outstanding ability to identify and recruit future leaders. Page was then serving as both chair of the MWSA Executive Board and president of the Brookline Woman Suffrage Association. Born in Ohio in 1860, she had enrolled as a special student at MIT before marrying and having four children. In the discouraging years after the 1895 referendum, Park later wrote, "[O]nly the courage of Alice Stone Blackwell and the energy of Mary Hutcheson" had kept MWSA going. The small number of remaining members had "occasional tea meetings" in their offices on the second floor of an old house on Park Street.[9]

Maud Wood Park at her Radcliffe graduation. *Courtesy of the Schlesinger Library, Radcliffe Institute, Harvard University.*

At Stone Blackwell's urging, Park attended NAWSA's convention in Washington, D.C., in 1900. She was dismayed to find that "[the first session] was held in the dreary basement vestry of a Washington church" with an audience of "about a hundred women, mostly middle-aged or elderly." When the state president from Missouri presented her report in verse, adjusting her pronunciation of the state's name to force rhymes, Park "became almost hysterical with suppressed laughter." Clearly, the national movement was in desperate need of a shake-up. Park decided to rescue the suffrage movement from what she called "the doldrums." Her weapon would be other college-educated women. She believed her peers owed a debt, which she called the "obligation of opportunity," to earlier women's rights activists whose efforts had made higher education and other opportunities available.[10]

Park and Inez Haynes co-founded the College Equal Suffrage League (CESL) in 1900. Park served as president and Haynes as corresponding secretary. The initial membership of twenty-five was drawn from alumnae of local colleges, including Radcliffe, Wellesley, and Boston University. The CESL's mission was to promote support for suffrage among alumnae and students and, nearly as important, to defeat indifference. Park found it "unthinkable that women who have learned to act for themselves in college and had their minds awakened to civic duties should not care for the ballot to enforce their wishes." She also lacked patience with those who felt they did not need the ballot because their own wishes were well met. "I think the majority of women do not realize how selfish, how unkind, this is," she commented. "It is as if a hungry woman had asked for food and another, more fortunate woman, had said to her, 'I will not give it to you because I have had a good breakfast and have all the food I want.'"[11]

The members of the CESL generated interest by holding regular meetings, sponsoring speeches and debates, circulating literature, organizing essay contests, and writing for college newspapers. The *Woman's Journal* helped by extensively publicizing CESL's efforts. Attuned to the boost that young, educated women could provide to the suffrage movement's image, Stone Blackwell wrote, "A pleasant fact is that most of the officers of the new League are remarkable not only for brains but for beauty, and beauty of a distinctively feminine type. There is not a mannish-looking woman among them."[12]

The CESL's membership grew rapidly. By 1906, there were more than 250 members, and by 1913, more than 450 women were members of the Massachusetts branch. Many students remained resistant or indifferent, however. Wellesley College conducted a poll to ascertain students' views in

" They ain't so awful mannish, Pop "

"They ain't so awful mannish, Pop," John Sloan, *Collier's*, May 18, 1912. *Courtesy of HathiTrust.*

1911. Only 293 students supported enfranchising women, while 557 were opposed and 528 did not participate.[13]

Showing the same resolve as the suffrage pioneers, Park tirelessly traversed the nation, encouraging the formation of new leagues of college students and alumnae. In 1905, she attended NAWSA's convention in Oregon and then traveled to Colorado, Idaho, Utah, and Wyoming to investigate the "practical working" of woman suffrage in the four states that had already adopted it. (Woman suffrage had returned to Utah in 1896, when it was admitted to statehood.) She returned with letters from numerous political and civic leaders praising the intelligence and morality of women voters. She used these to rebut the claims of suffrage opponents that political equality for women had been a "disaster" in the states where it existed.[14]

Park seldom confided the pressures she faced, but a letter from February 1906 reveals her burdens. She wrote, "I'm behind with my work, which always makes me out of sorts, and today I'm really ill with what I fancy is tonsillitis, though I don't dare to have the doctor for fear she'll tell me to stay in bed." After describing her "frightful" upcoming schedule of speeches, she continued, "and today my throat is so bad that I can only whisper."[15]

The college movement proved so successful that NAWSA's 1906 annual convention in Baltimore included a College Evening featuring a representative from each of the Seven Sister schools. (In addition to the four in Massachusetts, the others were Barnard, Bryn Mawr, and Vassar.) Park delivered an address urging college students and alumnae to persuade other college-educated women to "realize their debt" to past activists and "make them understand that one of the ways to pay that debt is to fight the battle in the quarter of the field in which it is still unwon." This convention also marked the final public appearance of Susan B. Anthony, who told the young and energetic recruits, "Failure is impossible."[16]

Delighted with the success of the CESL, NAWSA asked Park to organize leagues in additional states. In 1907, she temporarily moved to San Francisco to organize there and in the Midwest. She had been widowed in 1904, and she secretly married Robert Hunter, an actor and theatrical agent, in 1908. She shared the fact of her remarriage with only her closest confidantes, later explaining that "my kind of work could be better done by a supposed widow than by a woman known to be married and therefore suspected of neglecting her husband."[17] Park's decision is another reminder that prominent suffragists needed to be forever conscious of avoiding accusations that suffrage was incompatible with ordinary domestic life.

By 1908, fifteen states had CESL leagues. At that year's NAWSA convention in Buffalo, New York, the CESL became a national organization. M. Carey Thomas, the pro-suffrage woman president of Bryn Mawr College, was elected president, and Park became second vice-president and chair of the organization committee. She left the country for the next two years, however. With financial support from Pauline Agassiz Shaw, a wealthy suffrage supporter from Massachusetts, Park traveled around the world with photographer Mabel Willard to study women in other countries. Park sent extensive reports that were published in the *Woman's Journal* and contributed to keeping American women informed about women's advances elsewhere. She returned to Massachusetts to resume suffrage work in 1910.

The CESL's influence on the suffrage movement was considerable. In addition to providing new energy and skills, college women gave the movement, as Park acknowledged, "a kind of intellectual prestige that was needed."[18] College leagues also had a decisive practical impact. In California, for example, the San Francisco College League, which Park started in 1907, campaigned vigorously in the successful 1911 state suffrage campaign.

The CESL was only one of the indefatigable Park's achievements. Starting in 1901, she led the new Boston Equal Suffrage Association for Good Government, which is discussed in the next chapter. It would transform the suffrage movement by piloting new campaign and outreach tactics.

WORKING-CLASS WOMEN

While the CESL reached out to college women, other activists forged a cross-class, cross-ethnic, and cross-religious alliance with working-class women. Support for suffrage grew as working women became persuaded that the ballot was essential to goals such as limiting the hours worked by mothers and children in factories (without reducing pay), providing adequate urban sanitation, and ensuring safety of food and water.

The foundation for this successful coalition had been laid during the late nineteenth century. The Women's Educational and Industrial Union was founded by physician Harriet Clisby in Boston in 1877. She recruited a small group of well-to-do idealistic women to finance and manage this groundbreaking organization dedicated to offering charitable, educational, and vocational assistance to urban working-class women, the vast majority of them immigrants.

The settlement house movement of the late nineteenth century was crucial in connecting reformers to the state's immigrant communities. Though most often associated with Chicago, where Jane Addams opened the influential Hull House, the movement also flourished in Boston and other cities. Pauline Agassiz Shaw, the funder of Park's around-the-world travels, was among the most important settlement house backers. The daughter of Harvard professor Louis Agassiz and stepdaughter of Radcliffe co-founder Elizabeth Cary Agassiz, she was married to Quincy Adams Shaw, one of the wealthiest men in Massachusetts.

As immigrants poured into the city, Shaw founded the North Bennett Street Industrial School and Civic House in Boston's North End in 1879. At these and other settlement houses, members of women's clubs and young college graduates joined forces to provide first- and second-generation Italian, Jewish, and Irish immigrants with job training, English-language skills, child care, healthcare, and other services. Settlement house work exposed privileged reformers to the practical concerns of wage-earning women.

The Women's Trade Union League, founded in 1903, represented a new stage in cross-class relations, as it brought together recently unionized women workers and wealthy philanthropists. Fittingly, principal founders Mary Kenney O'Sullivan and Mary Morton Kimball Kehew had starkly different backgrounds. Kehew's maternal grandfather had been governor of Massachusetts, her father was a banker, and her husband was a wealthy oil merchant.

In contrast, O'Sullivan was born to Irish Catholic immigrants in Missouri in 1864. Starting at age fourteen, she worked at bookbinderies in Missouri, Iowa, and then Chicago. Convinced that women must organize to improve working conditions, she established a union of women bookbinders in Chicago. Unionizing working women was challenging work. Many of them eschewed unionization, as they anticipated quitting their jobs after marriage. In 1888, less than 2 percent of the female workforce was organized into trade unions.[19] O'Sullivan's efforts were supported by Jane Addams, who offered the use of Hull House for labor meetings. Samuel Gompers, the first president of the American Federation of Labor (AFL), founded in 1886, hired O'Sullivan as the first national woman organizer in 1892. At this early stage, however, the AFL had little interest in working women and did not renew her contract.

Kehew invited O'Sullivan to Boston, where they discussed forming an alliance to press for higher wages and improved working conditions for women laborers. O'Sullivan also met her future husband on that visit and moved to Boston in 1894. She joined the board of the Women's Educational and Industrial Union and, with Kehew, founded an auxiliary Union for Industrial Progress to encourage trade unionism among women. O'Sullivan led or assisted unionization efforts among women bookbinders, laundresses, garment workers, rubber workers, and others. She and her family lived in the Denison Settlement House. She was widowed in 1902 when her husband, an AFL organizer and *Boston Globe* labor editor (and former streetcar driver), was killed in a streetcar accident.

The following year, O'Sullivan, Kehew, and several others decided to found a national organization to support trade unionism among women. The AFL was by then paying renewed attention to the potential strength that working women could bring to the labor movement, although it remained wary that women workers might exert downward pressure on wages. O'Sullivan announced the formation of the Women's Trade

Union League (WTUL) at the AFL's national convention held in Boston's Faneuil Hall in November 1903.[20] The WTUL would be an umbrella organization of women's trade unions dedicated to supporting existing labor unions, aiding the formation of new ones, and advancing legislation to improve pay and working conditions. Reflecting its cross-class character, Kehew was elected national president and O'Sullivan became secretary and first vice-president. Local branches of the WTUL were quickly organized in Boston, Chicago, New York, and other cities.

Mary Kenney O'Sullivan. *Courtesy of Schlesinger Library, Radcliffe Institute, Harvard University.*

O'Sullivan believed that all productive members of society have a natural right to vote and that women's inability to vote was directly responsible for wage and other disparities between male and female workers. Though NAWSA had not historically sought common ground with working women, that now changed. Some influential suffragists, including Jane Addams and other supporters of the settlement house movement, agreed that wage-earning women urgently needed the ballot. These suffragists were eager to form a bridge connecting the suffrage and labor movements, and they criticized the suffrage movement's historic ethnic and class prejudices. Some in NAWSA substantively agreed, and others recognized the practical advantages of an alliance. In 1906, when NAWSA representatives made what had become their annual visit to Capitol Hill to speak before the Senate Committee on Woman Suffrage, Mary Kenney O'Sullivan was included among the small number of presenters.[21]

The WTUL established a suffrage department in 1908. NAWSA and the WTUL sent delegates to each other's national conventions, and the WTUL urged working women to participate in suffrage rallies. For working women who felt uncomfortable in the middle- and upper-class ambiance of NAWSA events, the WTUL established wage-earners' suffrage leagues. NAWSA president Anna Howard Shaw hired leading New York labor organizer Rose Schneiderman to persuade working women of the necessity to vote.

In a bow to the changing times, NAWSA ended its support of educational qualifications for voting in 1909.[22]

Those in NAWSA who supported an alliance with working-class women typically also favored an alliance with working-class men who, of course, could demonstrate their support by voting for woman suffrage. O'Sullivan and the WTUL helped strengthen that still-tentative connection between rank-and-file union men and the cause of woman suffrage. In a NAWSA pamphlet entitled "Why the Working Woman Needs the Vote," O'Sullivan argued that women's votes would directly benefit working-class men. She explained that low wages for women exerted downward pressure on men's wages because an employer could hire an inexpensive woman laborer in place of a man. With the ballot, she contended, women would have the power to demand higher wages. She was also careful to stress that suffrage would not disturb ordinary domestic life. She explained that women's higher wages would not be a "hardship" for men because "the increase in the man's wages will give the family the large income needed, without its being necessary for so many women to work outside the home."[23]

O'Sullivan's Catholicism also eased Catholics' historical distrust of the suffrage movement. Many male union members—nearly all Democrats and many of them Catholic—believed that women would support such Progressive Era reforms as the campaign for an eight-hour workday and a minimum wage. In 1907, AFL head Gompers told Anna Howard Shaw that his organization was committed to "equal suffrage, equal rights, and equal pay," and by 1909, 235 unions in Massachusetts had endorsed woman suffrage.[24] Thus, through its alliance with the WTUL, the woman suffrage movement was able finally to attract more working-class Democrats to its cause.

AFRICAN AMERICAN WOMEN

Even before the turn-of-the-century focus on college and working-class women, Boston's African American women had already moved in a new direction. In 1890, Josephine Ruffin, whose husband died in 1886, had begun organizing Boston's black women to combat both gender- and race-based discrimination. At the time, she was a journalist writing for the *Courant*, a weekly paper serving Boston's black community.

Ruffin decided to form a club for black women in Boston, though white women were not prohibited from joining. Her own civic involvements, including membership in the New England Women's Club, had given her firsthand knowledge of the way such clubs nurtured sisterhood and promoted good works. In 1893, Ruffin and her daughter, Florida Ruffin Ridley, a Boston schoolteacher, founded the Women's Era Club. By March 1894, over one hundred black women had joined the club with the uplifting motto, "Help to make the world better." Club members were literate and largely drawn from families that held positions of influence within the local black community.[25]

The following year, Ruffin, Ridley, and Maria Baldwin, a black school principal in Cambridge, founded the *Woman's Era*, a monthly newspaper. In the editors' opinion, the paper responded to the need for a "medium of intercourse and sympathy between the women of all races and conditions" but especially "of the educated and refined, among the colored women, members of which class may be found in every state from Maine to Florida."[26]

From the outset, the *Woman's Era* made clear that it would focus on race as well as gender. It opposed racial discrimination and supported black journalist Ida Wells Barnett's campaign against lynching of black men in the South. It did not spare NAWSA from criticism, protesting the choice of Atlanta as a site for the 1895 convention and its acquiescence to the racist demands of white southerners.[27]

Ruffin ambitiously decided to form a national federation of black women's clubs. To this end, the Woman's Era Club invited representatives from other black women's clubs to convene in Boston in July 1895. Approximately two hundred women from twenty clubs in ten states attended. The purpose of the convention was to address issues of "vital importance to us as women, but also the things that are of special interest to us as [black] women." Taking direct aim at those who claimed that black women were morally inferior to white women—a common accusation of white racists—Ruffin announced that a federation would teach "an ignorant and suspicious world that our aims and interests are identical with those of all good aspiring women."[28]

Attendees founded the Federation of African-American Women, which, following a subsequent merger, became the National Association of Colored Women, headed by Mary Church Terrell. (It later became the National Association of Colored Women Clubs (NACW).) Black women's clubs supported the suffrage movement, which they considered part of a larger battle for civil rights, and the NACW established a suffrage department to educate members about the benefits of suffrage. NAWSA, however, did not welcome black clubs. Discriminatory racial attitudes continued to

Josephine St. Pierre Ruffin.
Courtesy of HathiTrust.

find widespread acceptance within NAWSA. The "unwritten and largely unspoken NAWSA policy" on black suffragists was to ignore them and, "if pressed, refuse their allegiance and aid."[29] The connection between race and gender discrimination remained severed.

Although the *Woman's Era* ceased publication in 1897 following an unsuccessful appeal for financial support and the Women's Era Club disbanded in 1903, Ruffin remained an activist and community leader for the remainder of her life. She waged her own public battle against racism in the white women's club movement. When the General Federation of Women's Clubs, which had formed in 1890, met in Milwaukee in 1900, Ruffin was part of the Massachusetts state delegation. Her application to attend as the president of the Women's Era Club had been accepted without the national organizers realizing that it was a club of African American women. The Federation president, who was from Georgia, refused to seat Ruffin as a representative of the Women's Era Club, but—seeking a quiet resolution—offered instead to seat her as a delegate from either the Massachusetts Federation of Women's Clubs or the New England Women's Press Club. Ruffin refused to accept this substandard treatment. She was supported by the Massachusetts Federation, which urged the General Federation to admit women's clubs regardless of members' "race, creed, or politics."[30] Two years later, the General Federation reached a compromise that gave each state federation authority over matters of membership.

Ruffin was a founding member of the Boston chapter of the NAACP in 1911. She continued to espouse the view that the struggles against racial and gender discrimination were linked, as they had been at their birth, and that each movement's successes would benefit the other. But these sentiments found little support among NAWSA's leaders. The efforts of black women suffragists remained part of a narrative of exclusion and separation.

8
NEW TACTICS

D ue to the extraordinary seed-sowing efforts of Maud Wood Park, Mary Kenney O'Sullivan, and their allies, Massachusetts suffragists regained the ground lost after the 1895 "sham referendum." By 1908, the Massachusetts Woman Suffrage Association claimed more than one hundred local affiliates and, with nearly twenty thousand members, more members than any state suffrage association except New York's.[1] The suffrage movement continued to adopt new tactics to broaden its appeal and visibility. Expanding beyond the lecture circuit and fundraising fair, activists moved "out of the parlor and into the streets" to reach new audiences.[2]

The Boston Equal Suffrage Association for Good Government (BESAGG) was central to these new efforts. The indomitable trio of Maud Wood Park, Mary Hutcheson Page, and Pauline Agassiz Shaw founded this organization in 1901 in order to combine efforts to secure suffrage with direct activities for civic improvement. Park served as executive secretary, Page chaired the board and the membership committee, and Shaw financed the organization and held the honorary title of president. Soon after BESAGG's formation, it became an auxiliary member of MWSA and admitted members residing from anywhere within the greater Boston area. By 1910, BESAGG claimed five hundred members.[3]

The new organization established committees charged with addressing popular Progressive Era topics such as public school improvement, civic sanitation, the prevention of vice, and the care of the poor and disabled. Suffrage work quickly eclipsed other efforts, however. Park explained that members shared "[t]he conviction that in a democracy the conscientious use of the ballot is the most direct way in which to work for good government."[4]

Several factors likely ignited BESAGG's decision to test new suffrage tactics. First were the activities of the English Women's Social and Political Union (WSPU), which was founded by Emmeline Pankhurst in 1903. It engaged in such "militant" forms of protest as holding public street meetings ("open-air" meetings), heckling speakers, and disrupting political meetings. The British press derogatorily dubbed WSPU members "suffragettes," and they adopted this moniker. The American press covered WSPU activities extensively, particularly in 1908, when Pankhurst was arrested for the first time as she sought to deliver a petition to the prime minister. At her trial, she declared to the judge, "We are not here because we are law-breakers; we are here in our efforts to become law-makers."[5] During the winter and spring of 1909, two English suffragettes visited Boston and discussed their use of open-air meetings to attract attention. In New York, Harriot Stanton Blatch and her Equality League of Self-Supporting Women were also experimenting with open-air meetings.[6]

Another factor was the success of an event that had taken place in the city of Lynn, Massachusetts, the previous September. Four members of the Lynn Equal Suffrage Association arrived in the center of town in an automobile, itself an eye-catching event. They were accompanied by several musicians whose playing quickly attracted a crowd. Soon, the suffragists were addressing a spontaneously gathered audience of several hundred. In the *Woman's Journal*, Henry Blackwell enthused, "This very successful meeting opens up a new method of popularizing woman suffrage, well worthy of imitation. Not ten of that large audience could have been persuaded to enter a church or hall."[7] At eighty-three, Blackwell was still an active suffragist, and he remained so until his death the following year.

BESAGG quickly adopted the tactic of open-air meetings. In the absence of Maud Wood Park, who was on her world tour, Susan Fitzgerald led the organization. She had worked at a New York settlement house after her graduation from Bryn Mawr College. After moving to Boston in 1906, she threw her formidable energy into both the suffrage and trade union campaigns. Page placed her at the helm of BESAGG.

Fitzgerald and three other suffragists held their first open-air meeting on Bedford's town common in June 1909. To publicize the event, they affixed large yellow posters in store windows and on signposts and telegraph poles in Bedford and nearby communities. An audience of nearly one hundred, the majority of them men, gathered as Fitzgerald stood on a wooden box and addressed passers-by. Her aides held "Votes for Women" signs and distributed leaflets.[8]

Suffragists held similar events on Wednesdays and Saturdays throughout the summer. Though town commons were the usual destination, the suffragists "occasionally varied the program by going to the beaches or on special excursions where [they] could catch the holiday crowd." Not surprisingly, the suffragists sometimes encountered resistance, but speakers responded with persistence and ingenuity. For example, when officials forbade suffragists from speaking on popular Nantasket Beach, they carried their "Votes for Women" banner into the water and "spoke from the sea to the audience on the shore."[9]

SOME NEW CAMPAIGNERS

Future leaders became involved through these new campaign efforts. Florence Luscomb, who had recently graduated from MIT with a degree in architecture, was born into an activist family in Worcester. When she was five, her mother took her to Washington, D.C., to hear Susan B. Anthony speak. At MIT, where she was 1 of 12 women in a student body of 1,200, Luscomb joined the College Equal Suffrage League and delivered speeches and distributed literature in support of suffrage. She attended the open-air meeting in Bedford and made her own open-air speaking debuts in the town of Dedham and the Hyde Park neighborhood of Boston. Her competition included "passing fire engines, elevated trains, hollering drunks and dog fights."[10]

Teresa Crowley, who was born in Wakefield in 1873, pursued an amateur career as an actress and worked as a secretary before marrying attorney John Crowley. After having three children, she became a lawyer. (Massachusetts had admitted its first woman lawyer to the bar in 1882.) She was recruited to the suffrage movement by Mary Hutcheson Page. Crowley began as a volunteer in BESAGG's office but soon became a commanding outdoor speaker. She appeared with Fitzgerald in Bedford. Historians have often identified Crowley as Irish Catholic (her maiden name was O'Leary), but the evidence suggests otherwise. Her sister and grandson emphasized that Crowley's mother was descended from "old colonial stock" and that her father, a successful businessman, was born in London. Her grandson reported that Crowley once wore orange (the color of Irish Protestants) to a gathering of Boston Irish Catholics, a mistake unlikely to be made by an Irish Catholic.[11]

Some of the newcomers did contribute to diversifying the suffrage movement. Jennie Loitman Barron, of Boston's West End, was the daughter of Russian Jewish immigrants committed to educating their four daughters. After graduating first in her class at Boston's Girls' High School, in 1906, she entered Boston University, where she founded the Boston University Equal Suffrage League. Another pioneering lawyer, she continued her education at Boston University Law School. Barron later recalled campaigning for suffrage from soapboxes and open automobiles, while "at times dodging such missiles as stale eggs and overripe tomatoes."[12]

Margaret Foley became a leader of efforts to reach out to working-class immigrants, especially Catholics. Born to a working-class Irish Catholic family in 1875, Foley attended public school in Dorchester. Her interest in woman suffrage began when "there was much talk at home about [her brother's] voting and future political affiliations," but her queries were met with laughter. In her teens, with a dream of a career as a music performer, she traveled to California, where she visited relatives while teaching gymnastics and swimming at resorts. Returning to Boston, she became a hat trimmer and joined the hat trimmers' union of the WTUL. She worked as a paid speaker and organizer for MWSA starting in 1906.[13]

TROLLEY TOURS AND NEW OUTREACH

Elated by the interest demonstrated by audiences at open-air meetings, Fitzgerald organized a statewide "trolley tour" in August 1909. Maintaining an exhausting pace, she and several others traveled west through northern towns and returned through southern towns.[14] Resting only on Sundays, the women delivered ninety-seven speeches and reached an estimated twenty-five thousand people. Luscomb described their modus operandi after arriving in a town and unloading a six-foot long "Votes for Women" banner and suitcases heavy with leaflets and buttons:

> *We make for the nearest drug store, deposit all our luggage in one corner, and to compensate for its storage, all of us are duty bound to buy sodas.... While we drink, the drug clerk is cross-examined as to where the best*

audience can be collected, time of trolleys, hotel for the night, factories and mills in town, number of employees, men or women, union or non-union.... Then our leaflets are unpacked, our flag erected, we borrow a Moxie box from the drug clerk and proceed to the busiest corner of the town square.

The speaker might address her initial remarks to "the air, three assorted dogs, six kids, and two loafers." As the others distributed handbills, the audience would increase from "25 to 500, according to the time and place."[15] At each stop, the activists recruited supporters to establish local headquarters and carry on the work.

Press reports of the trolley tour were largely positive. Local papers described the speakers as attractive in appearance, refined, intelligent, and able to command the attention of mostly male audiences. Alice Stone Blackwell reprinted these accolades for the *Woman's Journal*'s national readership. The trolley tour ended with a large meeting held on Boston Common that was attended by two thousand.[16]

Foley, meanwhile, addressed factory workers during their noon break and attended union meetings in the evenings. She had a special rapport with working-class women, to whom she appealed as both workers and homemakers. On the one hand, she argued that only the ballot would improve working conditions. On the other, she insisted that mothers must have a voice in selecting those officials who made sure that milk and water were pure, meat and canned goods were not poisonous, clothing was not insect-infested, and parks and playgrounds were safe.[17]

The suffrage movement also continued its outreach to society women. Alva Belmont hosted a NAWSA meeting and fundraiser at Marble House, her magnificent summer villa in Newport, Rhode Island. For the event, she ordered dinnerware imprinted with "Votes for Women." Honored guests included ninety-one-year-old Julia Ward Howe. Susan Fitzgerald and Margaret Foley were also part of the Massachusetts contingent.[18]

The finale of the 1909 campaign season was Emmeline Pankhurst's visit to Boston in October, the initial stop on her first U.S. tour. Alice Stone Blackwell used the *Woman's Journal* to allay concern that Pankhurst's "militancy" would harm recent efforts to broaden suffrage's appeal. Stone Blackwell explained that the WSPU had heckled politicians and disrupted government meetings only after women were denied the ability to deliver petitions to and meet with government officials. "Nine-tenths of so-called militant tactics have been neither illegal nor violent, and might be used in this country with great advantage," she remarked.[19]

When Pankhurst arrived, she was escorted from South Station in a procession of automobiles decorated in the colors of the two movements: yellow for NAWSA and purple, white, and green for the WSPU. Speaking to an audience of two thousand at Tremont Temple, she noted that while her tactics might not be polite, neither were those of the Boston patriots who had thrown British tea into the harbor. Delightedly, the *Woman's Journal* reported that applause at the close of her remarks was "most enthusiastic."[20]

Inez Haynes wrote to Park, who was still abroad, that "the movement, which when we got into it had about as much energy as a dying kitten, is now a big, virile, threatening, wonderful thing." It was, she added, "actually fashionable."[21] NAWSA sought to harness this new vitality; it held a symposium on open-air techniques at its 1910 convention, and the *Woman's Journal* published Susan Fitzgerald's remarks to share with a national audience.[22]

During the warm-weather months of 1910, Massachusetts suffragists held large numbers of open-air meetings at town commons, factories, and street corners. They rented a storefront on Tremont Street and served literature and speakers along with lunch and afternoon tea.[23] As they campaigned, suffragists forged great friendships. Trolley tours and other forms of campaigning were liberating—and fun—for women who traveled without male escorts.[24]

Automobiles permitted even greater freedom. The suffrage movement used cars for transportation but also as "public platform, object for ritual decoration, and emblem of the cause of women's emancipation."[25] Some campaigners experimented with even bolder techniques. In Lawrence, Foley rose in a hot-air balloon and showered rainbow-colored literature on the crowd. In Brockton, suffragists joined a circus parade in a decorated wagon. Such high-profile stunts assured a steady stream of press coverage. [26]

BESAGG also created the Woman Suffrage Party, which was not a traditional political party but rather a vehicle to reach, recruit, and organize women who resided in Boston. Modeled after a similar undertaking in New York, the ambitious goal of the party was to reach every voting-age woman in the city and identify her as pro-suffrage, anti-suffrage, or indifferent. Those identifying as supporters were asked to join the Woman Suffrage Party, whose tightly organized structure included ward chairs and precinct captains. The hope was that pro-suffrage members would influence their husbands, sons, brothers, and fathers. [27]

This method was piloted in Boston's Ward 8, where many Jewish and Italian families lived. Urban canvassing was another new adventure for

Margaret Foley in a hot-air balloon at a suffrage rally. *Courtesy of Schlesinger Library, Radcliffe Institute, Harvard University.*

most suffragists. "It took some sense of duty, some devotion to our cause, to push us through the first unguarded front door, up the dim and unattractive staircase, to knock at [a] door on the first shabby landing," Susan Fitzgerald wrote in a BESAGG Annual Report. When the door was opened, "probably

Suffragists in Copley Square, 1910. *Courtesy of Schlesinger Library, Radcliffe Institute, Harvard University.*

the woman who answered knew no English....No matter, you did as well as you could, the children, who have learned English, helped; the Yiddish and Italian flyers helped." Best of all, "the women, as soon as they knew what it was all about, proved so kindly, so approachable, so open-minded and responsive to the call of fair play and their children's welfare."[28]

These door-to-door efforts were followed by postcards in several languages inviting women to attend public meetings. The first one, held in a ward room in May 1910, was a resounding success. Approximately one thousand women attended. They represented at least "four or five nationalities" and spoke several languages, including Italian and Yiddish, reported the *Boston Globe*. All were, the article added, "hardworking, serious women" who listened closely to all that was said. Speakers addressed the crowd in several languages from a platform decorated with American flags and "Votes for Women" banners. [29]

Park returned to Boston at the end of the summer of 1910 and resumed her leadership of BESAGG. She also lectured regularly about her travels. Discussing women's experiences in other nations, she believed, helped to draw in audiences of the curious but not yet committed. Demonstrating increased attention to woman suffrage, the *Boston Globe* ran a large feature article describing her travels.[30] Upon Park's return, Mary Hutcheson Page orchestrated some personnel shifts. Park succeeded Alice Stone Blackwell as chair of the board of MWSA so the older woman could focus her efforts on the *Woman's Journal*, which moved into new quarters on Boylston Street in the new and thriving Back Bay neighborhood of Boston. (After her father's death in 1909, Stone Blackwell was the sole editor of the paper.) Fitzgerald became the executive secretary of MWSA; the previous year, she had been elected to succeed Stone Blackwell as NAWSA's recording secretary.[31]

The suffrage movement received a big lift on November 8, 1910, when Washington ended the long drought and became the first state to enfranchise women since Idaho in 1896. Suffragists hoped momentum from this victory would aid the vote in California scheduled for the following year.

During 1911, Massachusetts suffragists continued their efforts. They canvassed additional Boston wards and enrolled nearly three thousand more women in the Woman Suffrage Party. Park established street corner amateur nights, where women new to public speaking would stand on corners and announce "why they want to vote and why they believe they have the right to vote and why they are determined that they will vote." Luscomb and other "newsies" sold the *Woman's Journal* on busy Boston street corners and subway stations in another effort to attract new subscribers and attention.[32]

Significantly, there was now a public show of support for woman suffrage among men. The Massachusetts Men's League for Woman Suffrage, modeled after a New York league, was created on

Florence Luscomb selling the *Woman's Journal. Courtesy of Schlesinger Library, Radcliffe Institute, Harvard University.*

April 29, 1910, with Francis Jackson Garrison, son of abolitionist William Lloyd Garrison, serving on the executive committee. Soon, the *Woman's Journal* reported its delight that "the officers and members of the Men's League for Woman Suffrage are taking a more and more active part in the work, with both voice and pen."[33]

Louis Brandeis was among the notable Massachusetts men who became public supporters. In 1908, the Jewish lawyer had won fame by persuading the U.S. Supreme Court to uphold an Oregon law restricting the number of hours women could work in laundries. Earlier in his career, Brandeis opposed woman suffrage, but his opinion had changed. He became convinced that "no class or section of the community is so wise or so just that it can safely be trusted to govern well other classes or sections."[34]

On October 10, 1911, the male voters of California narrowly approved an amendment to the state constitution enfranchising women. Ecstatic suffragists held a victory celebration at Faneuil Hall. Park exclaimed, "I'm just standing on my head with joy!" The nation's suffrage constellation now had six stars.[35]

Later that fall, Pankhurst returned to the United States. Since her earlier visit, the English suffrage movement had entered a darker phase. On "Black Friday," November 18, 1910, police assaulted numerous suffragettes when they protested Parliament's refusal to consider a bill that would have extended the vote to property-owning women. Shortly thereafter, Pankhurst's younger sister, Mary Jane Clarke, was arrested for window-smashing. When her demand to be treated as a political prisoner was denied, Clarke went on a hunger strike. Prison officials retaliated by force-feeding her, a harrowing ordeal. She was released after serving one month in prison but died three days later.

During this visit, Pankhurst again spoke at Tremont Temple. Sharing a platform with Alice Stone Blackwell and Maud Wood Park, Pankhurst observed that the United States now had a "thoroughly alive" suffrage movement. She was also scheduled to speak at Harvard at a lecture sponsored by the Harvard Men's League for Woman Suffrage. When the resistant Harvard administration refused to permit use of a university-owned building, Pankhurst spoke at nearby Brattle Hall. Stone Blackwell deemed the visit a resounding success, writing that the lectures had done more to arouse interest in the suffrage movement than anything else in the United States.[36]

Though very busy with their home state efforts, Massachusetts activists also continued to play important national and even international roles.

Pauline Agassiz Shaw anonymously provided substantial funds to NAWSA; these donations permitted president Anna Howard Shaw (no relation) to pay organizers to travel to Arizona, Kansas, Oregon, Wisconsin, Michigan, North Dakota, Montana, Ohio, and Nevada.[37] BESAGG, likely with funds donated entirely or largely by Pauline Agassiz Shaw, sponsored Luscomb and Foley to travel to England to study the English suffrage movement and to Sweden to attend the International Woman Suffrage Alliance Convention. Park, Luscomb, Foley, Fitzgerald, and others campaigned extensively in other states, such as Ohio and Michigan, where voters would soon consider referenda. Luscomb additionally spent one week in Richmond, Virginia, where, she reported, southern suffragists sought her expertise, but "at the same time couldn't bear to be told anything by a damn Yankee."[38]

While these years were filled with progress, suffrage opponents had not disappeared into the sunset. Conservative remonstrants were as determined as ever to uphold the status quo. The *Remonstrance* had shifted from an annual to a quarterly publication schedule in 1907 and now represented suffrage opponents in seven other states. Remonstrants presented familiar arguments. They claimed that the suffrage movement "confused" the functions of men and women to the detriment of domestic life, reform-minded women could accomplish their goals most effectively if they remained removed from partisan battles, and it was "undemocratic" for suffragists to demand that the burden of politics be thrust on women until a majority of women demonstrated that they desired the ballot.

Deep opposition also remained among many working-class rank and file despite union leaders' alliance with the suffrage movement. Many workers remained wedded to traditional gender roles and feared that women workers would drive wages downward. The Catholic community's leading newspaper, the *Pilot*, continued to be vehemently anti-suffrage. Anti-prohibition forces also continued to oppose suffrage.

Despite continued challenges, 1911 marked a turning point. Growing numbers of Massachusetts state legislators now favored fully enfranchising women. The strong alliance between Democratic politicians and labor leaders led a majority of delegates at a state Democratic convention to endorse woman suffrage. The state Republican Party was nearly evenly split, reflecting its continued division. Displaying new confidence, MWSA sent men seeking office a questionnaire soliciting their views on woman suffrage. The *Boston Globe* reported that candidates were "beginning to believe this to be an issue which must be treated seriously, and that his position on the matter may mean his election or failure to secure office."[39] During the

Anti-suffrage cartoon. "Looking backward." Laura E. Foster, *Life* magazine, August 22, 1912. *Courtesy of the Library of Congress.*

1911 gubernatorial campaign, Margaret Foley tailed Republican candidate Louis Frothingham, who refused to support woman suffrage and who lost to Democratic incumbent Eugene Foss.[40] While his loss may have been for other reasons, Foley's acts brought additional public attention to the woman suffrage campaign. Though many challenges remained, Bay State suffragists were optimistic as 1912 began. They had good reason to believe that the suffrage tide would soon cross the Mississippi River and surge east.

9

A Second National Schism

To provide context for the next stage of the Massachusetts suffrage story, it is necessary to return to the national narrative. Woman suffrage became a national campaign issue for the first time during the presidential election of 1912. Women voters, now in six western states, had the potential to determine the outcome. Moreover, as woman suffrage seemed to spread to contiguous states once it gained a foothold, politicians in neighboring western states had reason to court potential future voters. Also influential was the support of popular former president Theodore Roosevelt, who ran as the presidential candidate of the new Progressive (Bull Moose) Party.

Roosevelt now endorsed woman suffrage despite not having done so while in office from 1901 to 1909. He was far from an egalitarian, but he had by now been persuaded by NAWSA that woman suffrage was no longer a radical proposition. Roosevelt announced he saw "no reason why voting should interfere with a woman's home life any more than it interferes with the everyday work of the man which enables him to support the home."[1] His endorsement demonstrates the success of NAWSA's rebranding as a moderate organization compatible with traditional gender roles under Catt's and Shaw's leadership.

Several prominent suffragists had important roles in Roosevelt's campaign. Jane Addams, the founder of Chicago's Hull House, seconded his nomination at the Progressive Party convention. Roosevelt appointed Maud Nathan, a Jewish woman from New York, to chair the Progressive

Party's Suffrage Committee. Her sister, Annie Nathan Meyer, was the founder of Barnard College in New York City and a prominent opponent of woman suffrage. Like Catharine Beecher and Sarah Josepha Hale, Meyer believed that women should be well educated but not enter the political sphere. As with the Beecher sisters, Meyer's and Nathan's shared upbringing and opposed viewpoints again illustrate the difficulty, if not impossibility, of historians' finding common factors able to predict which women would embrace suffrage and which would resist it.

The Republican and Democratic parties did not follow Roosevelt's lead. Incumbent William Howard Taft, the Republican nominee, promised to support suffrage only when there was a "substantial call" from women.[2] New Jersey governor Woodrow Wilson, the Democratic candidate, was an ardent opponent of woman suffrage, though on the campaign trail he maintained that he was undecided. Wilson won the presidency with 42 percent of the popular vote when the Republican vote was divided between Taft and Roosevelt.

Wilson may have triumphed, but the woman suffrage movement nevertheless emerged a winner. The voters of Oregon, Kansas, and Arizona approved amendments enfranchising women. Despite losses in Ohio, Michigan, and Wisconsin, women could now vote in nine states, all of them west of the Mississippi River. In a separate movement toward expansion of the franchise, Congress enacted the Seventeenth Amendment, which provided for the direct, popular election of U.S. senators. Ratification was completed in 1913. (Earlier that year, the Sixteenth Amendment, which provided for a federal income tax, had also been adopted.)

Soon after the 1912 election, Alice Paul and Lucy Burns, friends and American veterans of the English suffrage movement, asked to chair NAWSA's long-dormant, unfunded Congressional Committee. NAWSA president Anna Howard Shaw agreed that the time was ripe. Her decision would have far-reaching consequences.

PROGRESS AND A SECOND SCHISM

Alice Paul was born in New Jersey in 1885 to parents active in the Hicksite Quaker Church, the liberal branch to which Lucretia Mott had belonged. Paul's mother was a member of NAWSA, and she and her daughter sometimes attended suffragist meetings together. Paul graduated from

Swarthmore College in 1905, worked briefly at a settlement house in New York City, and earned a master's degree in sociology from the University of Pennsylvania. In 1907, she went to England to continue her studies and work among the poor. There, she joined Emmeline Pankhurst's Women's Social and Political Union (WSPU).

Burns was born in New York in 1879 to an affluent Irish Catholic family. She graduated from Vassar College and taught high school in Brooklyn before studying at the University of Berlin and Oxford University. She worked as a full-time salaried organizer for WSPU. She and Paul became friends and allies after they were both arrested for participating in a suffrage protest.

While in Great Britain, Paul was arrested seven times and sentenced to prison three times. During each incarceration, she joined hunger strikes called to protest the government's refusal to treat suffragettes as political prisoners. The first two led to her early release. The third time, British authorities ordered her to be forcibly fed through a tube placed in her nostril. Weakened by this dreadful ordeal, she returned to the United States in January 1910. She earned a PhD in sociology from the University of Pennsylvania in 1912, the same year that Burns returned to the United States.

Paul and Burns intended to use NAWSA's Congressional Committee to shift the organization's focus away from education, persuasion, and state campaigns and toward using women's increased political clout to secure a federal woman suffrage amendment. They believed the time was ripe, now that "one-fifth of the Senate, one-seventh of the House, and one-sixth of the electoral vote [came] from Suffrage States."[3] Their hero was the recently deceased Susan B. Anthony, and they referred to a woman suffrage amendment as "the Anthony amendment." They also brought a new strategy to the United States, one borrowed from the English WSPU. In opposition to NAWSA's nonpartisan stance, they pledged to hold the party in power (the Democrats) responsible for inaction on the proposed amendment. They insisted that suffrage supporters should vote against all Democrats regardless of whether an individual Democratic candidate supported woman suffrage.

To raise the national profile of the suffrage movement, Paul and Burns planned a massive parade on March 3, 1913, the day preceding President-elect Woodrow Wilson's inauguration. Like open-air meetings, parades marked a daring new phase in suffrage activities. Well-behaved women were not expected to make public spectacles of themselves.[4] Paul and Burns intended the parade to demonstrate the grandeur and gravity of the suffrage

Alice Paul. *Courtesy of the Library of Congress.*

movement to the thousands of influential people and journalists who would attend the inauguration.

Working intensely for several months, the two recruited funds, a small army of dedicated volunteers, and thousands of marchers. Paul and Burns shared NAWSA's desire to separate gender- and race-based discrimination and avoid antagonizing white southerners. They instructed black women to march in a segregated section in the rear of the parade.

The elaborate parade was led by Inez Milholland, who wore a flowing white cape and sat astride a white horse. Behind her followed nine bands, over twenty floats, several mounted brigades, and eight thousand marchers organized by state and occupation. Florence Luscomb and Mary Hutcheson Page were among those marching in the Massachusetts delegation. Ida B. Wells-Barnett of Chicago, the nation's foremost anti-lynching activist, refused to march in the rear but joined the white Illinois delegation after the parade had begun.

The participants soon encountered crowds of unruly men determined to block their way. While police "stood by with folded arms and grinned,"

Official program, Woman Suffrage Procession, Washington, D.C., 1913. *Courtesy of the Library of Congress.*

marchers were "spit upon, slapped in the face, tripped up, pelted with burning cigar stubs, and insulted by jeers and obscene language too vile to print or repeat."[5] The marchers soldiered on. Ultimately, the secretary of war ordered federal cavalry to restore order.

Admiration for the dignified and dedicated marchers, combined with anger at disruptive protestors and their police enablers, brought a wave of positive publicity to the suffrage movement. "Capital Mobs Made Converts to Suffrage," and "Parade Called Boon to Women...Insults Said to Have Made Friends" proclaimed headlines in the *New York Tribune* and the *Boston Globe*, respectively. Journalist Nellie Bly headlined her article for the *New York Evening Journal* "Suffragists Are Men's Superiors."[6]

This triumph was accompanied, however, by a new schism in the suffrage movement. Paul and Burns had founded a separate organization, the Congressional Union for Woman Suffrage, to support the activities of the unfunded Congressional Committee. Any interested woman could pay twenty-five cents to join the Congressional Union. They also established their own weekly newspaper, *The Suffragist*. In the December 1913 issue, the Congressional Union announced that it had adopted its own color scheme of purple, white, and gold. "Purple is the color of loyalty...to a cause... white, the emblem of purity, symbolizes the quality of our purpose; and gold, the color of light and life, is as the torch that guides our purpose."[7]

In response to these initiatives, NAWSA president Shaw demanded that Paul and Burns resign from the Congressional Union. Shaw complained that many understandably confused the Congressional Committee with the Congressional Union and declared that any funds raised by the Congressional Union belonged to NAWSA. In addition, she accused the Congressional Union of breaching NAWSA's longstanding protocol by organizing in states without an invitation from the state association. She also demanded that Paul and Burns abandon the policy of holding all Democrats responsible for inaction on a federal suffrage amendment. NAWSA maintained that this technique, while suitable in a parliamentary system, made no sense in the United States, where support for suffrage did not divide along party lines.

When the two younger women refused to comply, Shaw and her board removed them from the Congressional Committee and denied the Congressional Union status as an auxiliary member of NAWSA. Once again, a schism had opened between the two leading woman suffrage organizations. NAWSA and the Congressional Union (which would be known as the National Woman's Party starting in 1917) would henceforth be bitter rivals, with each convinced that the other was an obstacle to progress. Alice Stone

Blackwell explained in the *Woman's Journal* that the two organizations had such divergent policies and methods that suffrage supporters will "have to make their choice and line up with one or the other."[8]

On March 19, 1914, the U.S. Senate voted on a woman suffrage amendment for the first time since 1887. Despite the schism, Carrie Chapman Catt acknowledged that Paul and her allies deserved credit for prompting this vote.[9] The measure was defeated 35–34. (A two-thirds majority is required to pass a federal constitutional amendment and send it to the states for ratification votes.) The vote broke down thusly: 21 Republicans voted in support and 12 in opposition, including both of Massachusetts' Republican senators, Henry Cabot Lodge and John Weeks; 14 Democratic senators voted in support and 22 in opposition; and 26 senators did not vote. Democratic opponents were concentrated in the one-party South, while half of the Republican opponents were from New England. When the House voted nine months later, 174 members supported the measure and 204 opposed it. Three of the 8 Massachusetts Republican representatives and 5 of 8 Democratic representatives supported the amendment.

While Paul and her allies pursued a federal amendment, NAWSA continued to provide funds, organizers and leaflets to state campaigns. Embracing new modes of outreach, NAWSA made a pro-suffrage movie, *Votes for Women*, which featured Anna Howard Shaw and opened in New York in 1912. Suffragists composed numerous songs to perform at rallies. The *Woman's Journal* boosted its circulation from four thousand to fifteen thousand.[10]

When Illinois passed a statute in 1913 permitting women to vote in presidential elections, suffragists heralded this first breakthrough east of the Mississippi River as a sign of women's growing political clout and a harbinger of future success. Suffrage was, announced Catt during a visit to Massachusetts, a "mighty incoming tide, which is sweeping all before it and cannot be stopped."[11]

Another important milestone was reached in June 1914, when the General Federation of Women's Clubs, now composed of over four thousand local clubs and one million women, endorsed woman suffrage. This result was the culmination of years of effort by suffrage proponents who finally persuaded a majority of delegates that the ballot was necessary to secure women's many municipal housekeeping initiatives.

Momentum continued when both Nevada and Montana enfranchised women in 1914. Margaret Foley, who spent two months in Nevada at the invitation of the Nevada Woman Suffrage Association, was credited as the "biggest force" leading to success. The daring Foley "donned the miner's costume to go 2500 feet below the ground to talk to these [miners] whom she couldn't reach in any other way." Her primitive accommodations included "sheds without any bedclothing" and hotels where only a canvas partition separated her from drunken miners. [12]

Meanwhile, suffragists in Massachusetts had continued their in-state campaign. Their efforts, coupled with the new national momentum, would finally persuade the Massachusetts state legislature to endorse a state constitutional amendment enfranchising women in 1914. Male voters in Massachusetts would decide its fate in November 1915.

THE REFERENDUM OF 1915

B y 1912, Massachusetts activists were no longer willing to settle for partial enfranchisement. They turned their attention to obtaining a state constitutional amendment enfranchising women. Success would require the support of the state legislature for two consecutive years, followed by ratification by a majority of voters—all of them male, of course.

State suffrage leaders piloted an aggressive new strategy in 1912, the year that woman suffrage had first become a national campaign issue. This time, they targeted prominent suffrage opponents for defeat. Susan Fitzgerald steered this effort with Teresa Crowley, the chair of the Massachusetts Woman Suffrage Association's Legislative Committee. The first target was Republican state senator Roger Wolcott, a vehement suffrage opponent who led the legislature's constitutional amendments committee. Knowing that anti-suffragists generally also opposed other progressive measures, Crowley compiled a record of Wolcott's "nay" votes that suffragists disseminated throughout his district. He was defeated, an opening salvo that other opponents would have to heed.

The next year, suffragists targeted state senate president Republican Levi Greenwood. Crowley prepared a leaflet identifying Greenwood's many votes against labor and other progressive measures, while Foley and others campaigned against him at factories and town greens. "Down Main Street her [Foley's] little open car would dash, with the flaming yellow Votes for Women banner streaming out, to pull up at the central square," Luscomb recalled. Spectators hurried to the scene to hear Foley's arguments, "roar with mirth at her repartee, and see her flashing Irish wit put to rout all would be hecklers." Greenwood, too, was defeated. Legislators now had notice, Luscomb reported, "that they could not expect to knife woman suffrage without reprisal."[1]

These efforts, coupled with labor leaders' strong support for woman suffrage, had the desired effect. In 1914, the state legislature passed the amendment by large margins: 168 in favor and only 39 opposed in the House, and 34 in favor and 2 opposed in the Senate.[2] Correctly forecasting repeated legislative success the following year, suffragists now concentrated their energy on the referendum campaign. Male voters would consider the referendum on November 2, 1915. Men in three other important northeastern states—New York, New Jersey, and Pennsylvania—would also decide whether suffrage was on a determined march from west to east.

Maud Wood Park, Teresa Crowley, Mary Hutcheson Page, and Gertrude Halladay Leonard—known as the "Big Four"—led the state referendum campaign.[3] Leonard, the chair of MWSA's Executive Committee, was born in Boston, educated in Boston public schools and the Boston Normal School, and taught in the city's public schools until her marriage. She then devoted herself to woman suffrage.

Thousands dedicated their energy to the campaign. Local chapters of the College Equal Suffrage League asked every woman with a college education to "liquidate" the debt owed to suffrage pioneers. Susan Fitzgerald helped to found the Political Equality League, which focused on reaching laboring men and women. Margaret Foley also campaigned extensively among workers. Alice Stone Blackwell supplied a steady stream of pro-suffrage literature to newspapers and organizers.

City and town suffrage associations mushroomed, growing from 138 in the spring of 1914 to 200 just before the vote. These local associations produced speakers and other volunteers. The latter were encouraged to complete pledge slips that permitted them to choose from a wide-ranging list of tasks, including distributing suffrage literature, wearing a suffrage button in plain sight, loaning one's house for a suffrage meeting, or urging male acquaintances to form a Men's League for Woman Suffrage.[4]

Inspired by the Washington, D.C. parade of 1913, Gertrude Halladay Leonard planned a large parade in Boston to kick off the referendum campaign. Many other parades also took place on May 2, 1914, which NAWSA designated National Suffrage Day. Leonard appealed to local associations to send large numbers of marchers, and thousands responded.

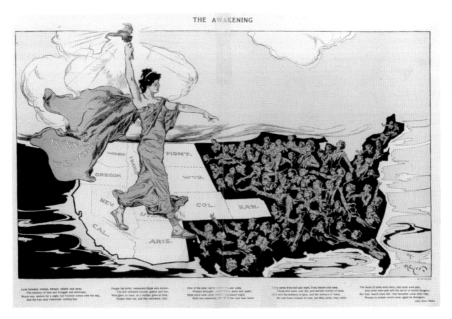

"The Awakening," Henry Mayer, *Puck*, February 20, 1915. *Courtesy of the Library of Congress.*

The elaborate parade included floats, bands, decorated cars, and more than twelve thousand marchers, most dressed in white. Marchers were grouped in many categories such as city women, country women, home women, business women, nurses, teachers, doctors, lawyers, farmers, wage-earning women, and college students. The Men's League for Suffrage marched, as did the descendants of a number of suffrage pioneers.[5]

A crowd of roughly 250,000 watched, and no significant disturbances were reported. The pro-suffrage *Boston Globe* gave extensive, positive front-page coverage to the parade, underscoring that "earnest marchers win favor with surging crowds." There were, of course, "antis" among the spectators, but the suffragists' yellow flowers and ribbons "utterly outshone" the antis' red roses. Governor David Walsh, who reviewed the parade as it passed the state house, remarked that this demonstration by dignified and intelligent women "will serve to attract more thought to the vital problem of equal suffrage." Contemplating the power of suffrage parades, Luscomb remarked that parades provided visual proof that the women who wanted suffrage were "ordinary, representative women—homemakers, mothers, daughters, teachers, working women—not the unsexed freaks the antis declared they were."[6]

Margaret Foley at the 1914 Boston parade. *Courtesy of Schlesinger Library, Radcliffe Institute, Harvard University.*

Suffragists worked to reach as many registered voters (and their wives) as possible. By the spring of 1915, MWSA employed 9 organizers and 5 speakers in the field and made an additional 125 women and 76 men available for speaking engagements. They reached people on street corners and at factories, stores, men's clubs, union meetings, church organizations, and county fairs. An army of volunteers canvassed 250,000 voters; of these, 100,000 signed pledge cards, and more than 50,000 others indicated they were favorable toward the referendum.[7] One canvasser described the hard work: "We left home very early every morning....We worked through until 9 or 9:30 in the evening....For the first three days the calves of our legs just ached and it was slow going." BESAGG relied on male canvassers in Italian neighborhoods, believing men would have more success there.[8]

The state's suffrage movement won a major victory when the Massachusetts State Federation of Women's Clubs, representing sixty-five thousand women, endorsed woman suffrage at its convention in June 1915.[9] Delighted supporters hoped that many women's club members would persuade their husbands and sons to support the referenda.

Suffragists continued to make effective use of automobile tours. Florence Luscomb organized auto tours in the eastern part of the state, while Agnes Morey covered the west. In each town, volunteers canvassed homes, distributed literature, and delivered speeches. For four months they worked "[t]hrough rain and shine, heat and cold, friendship and hostility." In central Massachusetts, Molly Dewson and her partner, Polly Porter, "relished the sensation they created as they cruised the Worcester countryside in a car covered with suffrage banners and emblems."[10] Julia O'Connor, the president of the Massachusetts branch of the Women's Trade Union League, led the Wage Women's Wedge's sponsorship of an auto tour by women union leaders.[11]

Maud Wood Park, always conscious of the debts modern women owed to their predecessors, made sure that Lucy Stone and other suffrage pioneers were celebrated during the campaign. Park spoke before a crowd in Boston Common on August 13, 1915, which would have been Lucy Stone's ninety-seventh birthday. The following day, suffragists converged on her birthplace in West Brookfield. In October, they celebrated the anniversary of the First National Women's Rights Convention. Luscomb drove Lucy Stone's carriage from Boston to Worcester, where there was an anniversary luncheon followed by a parade and evening rallies. Florence Seaver Slocomb, a suffragist and president of the Worcester Women's Club, was a key organizer of these events.[12]

Black leaders in Massachusetts supported the referendum, although they supported an attack on both race and sex discrimination.[13] W.E.B. Du Bois, who edited the NAACP's journal *The Crisis*, devoted the August 1915 issue to a symposium by black leaders on suffrage. The magazine's cover featured both Sojourner Truth and Abraham Lincoln to stress the historical connections between race and gender discrimination. Josephine Ruffin, who contributed to the issue, praised many leaders in the woman suffrage movement as "farsighted" and "broadminded" and offered her opinion that the black community was justified in believing that woman suffrage would mean more progress toward racial equality.[14]

Many in the Jewish community supported the referendum. In a rally held at Boston's Temple Israel, Rabbi Henry Levy said that he was a suffragist because "Judaism is democratic and democracy must include woman suffrage."[15] As Jennie Loitman Barron vigorously campaigned, she debunked the myth that women who inhabited the domestic sphere should not vote:

> *If you men should ask us for the vote, should we say, Mr. Carpenter, "your sphere is at the bench"; Mr. Blacksmith, "your place is at the forge"; Mr. Chauffeur, "your place is in the garage"; Mr. Clerk, "your place is in the shop and therefore you should not have the ballot."…*[T]*hat would be as absurd an objection as to argue that "women's place is in the home" should disqualify her to vote.*[16]

Suffragists targeted the Catholic community through posters and leaflets that showcased prominent clergy praising woman suffrage in the states and nations that had enfranchised women. For example, Father Joseph Gleason of California declared that as a Catholic priest, he found "no danger to the dignity of womanhood or motherhood to be feared from the ballot." Archbishop Francis Redwood of New Zealand announced, "Women have had the vote in New Zealand for many years, and it has been proven that they use it wisely and judiciously, and for the greatest common good."[17]

Suffrage supporters were elated when each of the five candidates for governor in the upcoming state election—representing the Democratic, Republican, Progressive, Socialist and Prohibitionist Parties—endorsed suffrage. They hoped that support at the top of each ticket would swell the number of men voting for the woman suffrage amendment. Supporters were jubilant when even President Woodrow Wilson announced his support for the New Jersey referendum (the state where he was registered to vote). His change of heart was due, at least in part, to the efforts of his daughter,

Tin bluebird designed by Florence Luscomb for the 1915 Massachusetts suffrage campaign. *Courtesy of the Sophia Smith Collection, Smith College.*

Margaret, whose support for suffrage was well known; she even served on an honorary NAWSA committee that year. Wilson explained that although he intended to vote for woman suffrage in New Jersey because "the time has come," he would be doing so as a private citizen and not in his capacity as the nation's president and the leader of the Democratic Party. He also reiterated that this "great question" was a matter for state governments only.

As Election Day approached, suffragists designed creative, high-profile activities intended to keep their cause in the public eye. On "Suffrage Bluebird Day" in July, volunteers placed 100,000 twelve-inch blue, white, and yellow tin bluebirds bearing the words "Votes for Women" around the state. On "Suffrage Day at Fenway Park," four hundred leaders and workers, wearing yellow sashes and carrying yellow pennants, attended a doubleheader as guests of the club's president. BESAGG held a "suffrage ball" at popular Revere Beach. Dances included the "suffrage glide" and the "votes-for-women two-step." Some suffragists also made time to support other states' campaigns. For example, Foley addressed fans before a baseball game in Philadelphia.[18]

Prominent suffragists from other states came to Massachusetts. NAWSA president Anna Howard Shaw visited Fall River, Lynn, Fitchburg, Newton, Brockton, and Lowell.[19] Other campaigners came from California, Nevada, and Idaho. They brought encouragement from states that had already granted women the vote.

Suffragists planned a second Boston parade to take place several weeks before election day. Optimistically called the Victory Parade, this October 16, 1915 parade was even larger than the one held the previous year. Thirty bands accompanied approximately fifteen thousand marchers. A new feature was a group of foreign-born young men and women marching under a New Americans banner. The Men's League for Suffrage again participated. Spectators numbered half a million, and the *Boston Globe* reported that this parade "sets a record for enthusiasm." At a mass rally held after the parade, Boston mayor Curley urged voters to enfranchise women. He reminded them that although Massachusetts was then arguably "the great conservative center" of the nation, history proved that "more radical steps had their birth here" than elsewhere.

Other communities also held parades, including Worcester and Springfield, where over one thousand women and men marched along a route where houses, stores, and businesses were "liberally decorated with suffrage flags and emblems, alternating with the Stars and Stripes."[20] The Worcester campaign closed with a dramatic torchlight parade on October 30.[21]

Despite all these efforts, victory remained a long uphill climb. The anti-suffragists were also out in force. Opponents began with two advantages: only men would be able to vote on the referendum, and the anti-suffrage campaign was very well financed. The Men's Anti-Suffrage Committee continued to be led by wealthy and influential men determined to avoid, as the anti-suffrage *New York Times* wrote, the "transform[ation] of the whole political and social fabric."[22] They feared, as they always had, that women voters would shirk their domestic duties, undermine men as heads of household, and support labor unions and prohibition.

The Massachusetts Association Opposed to the Further Extension of Suffrage to Women, now renamed the Woman's Anti-Suffrage Association of Massachusetts, continued to be led by women married to prominent men. That organization claimed a membership of over 35,000 women across the state. Remonstrants again maintained that men should not enfranchise women until such time as women proved that a majority of women sought it. The Woman's Anti-Suffrage Association ran ads claiming that fewer than 10 percent of Massachusetts women demanded the ballot. As "proof," remonstrants cited the results of the 1895 referendum and the low turnout by women in school committee elections. Suffragists countered with reminders that after years of effort, remonstrants claimed as supporters only thirty-six thousand of over one million women of voting age in Massachusetts, leaving—suffragists claimed—over one million women not opposed to suffrage.

Remonstrants also continued to claim that suffragists were dangerous radicals. They ran ads accusing woman suffrage of being part of the "feminist movement" and "wanted by every Socialist, every IWW, and every

Mormon." Remonstrants urged voters not to "join hands with these enemies of the home and of Christian civilization." Suffragists retorted that while some radicals might support suffrage, the converse was not true.[23]

Women opponents did not initially campaign "in the streets." They established storefronts plastered with anti-suffrage posters. They also spoke at women's clubs and hosted booths at county fairs throughout the state. As the election approached, however, some remonstrants used the tactics of suffragists. In late September, members of the Woman's Anti-Suffrage Association left Boston for a five-week automobile tour of the state, with rallies scheduled in every city and nearly every town. The *Boston Globe* noted, "The speaking at the open-air rallies will be by men only, but men and women together will take part in the evening programs."[24]

Many members of the working class clung to tradition and continued to oppose woman suffrage despite the pleas of labor leaders. The *Pilot* newspaper continued its opposition. Moreover, longstanding fears among many Catholics that the ballot would undermine the family received new life when the birth control movement began. Margaret Sanger, herself an Irish Catholic, launched a newsletter promoting contraception in 1914, and the National Birth Control League was founded in 1915. There were close ties between the birth control and suffrage movements. For example, Mary Ware Dennett, one of the founders of the National Birth Control League, had previously served as field secretary of MWSA and corresponding secretary of NAWSA.

The anti-suffrage campaign gained momentum when New Jersey defeated its referendum on October 19, 1915. (Massachusetts, New York, and Pennsylvania would all vote on November 2.) This defeat was a powerful reminder that many men remained unwilling to share power with women. Despite their disappointment over the New Jersey result, suffrage supporters in Massachusetts urged voters to demonstrate that the "eternal principles of liberty, justice, and equality for which [their] forefathers died, are still a living thing in Massachusetts."[25]

On November 2, 1915, eight thousand women stood for hours at polling locations throughout the state holding placards reading, "Show Your Faith in the Women of Massachusetts: Vote 'Yes' on Woman Suffrage." Park spent the day journeying from one precinct to another offering encouragement. Meanwhile, saloons passed out pink slips reading "Good for two drinks if woman suffrage is defeated."[26]

In the end, the old abolitionist stronghold of Massachusetts refused to extend rights to women. It was a crushing defeat: men cast nearly 325,000 "no" votes, and fewer than 133,000 "yes" votes. The referendum was defeated in every city and town except the small southeastern town of Berkeley. The referenda were also defeated in New York and Pennsylvania, but the largest margin of defeat was in Massachusetts.[27] The Bay State continued to have a sizable faction of conservative Republicans out of step with the national party. Furthermore, the alliance between the Democratic Party and labor leaders had failed to sway many rank-and-file working-class voters.

Massachusetts suffragists had been leaders in the movement since its inception. Their efforts had helped enfranchise women elsewhere, but they were unable to translate their work into a victory in their own home state. It's difficult to know whether activists, many of whom had dedicated years to the campaign, were surprised by their loss. Many years later, Park wrote, "My own opinion about the submission of the Massachusetts woman suffrage amendment—an opinion which I tried to keep to myself—was that we had little or no chance…though I hoped for a creditable showing which would pave the way for future success."[28]

At least publicly, leaders remained positive, viewing defeats in the four northeastern states as a temporary "interruption" in the steady march toward ultimate victory. MWSA leaders pledged support for a new campaign, as did leaders from New York, New Jersey, and Pennsylvania. Alice Stone Blackwell emphasized that over one million men in the four states had supported women, and called the minority vote "the handwriting on the wall."[29] But the movement was at another crossroads. Like the defeat of the Massachusetts municipal suffrage referendum in 1895, the 1915 defeats in the Northeast triggered transformative changes in the movement. NAWSA would decide that the extensive support for woman suffrage in the West, combined with the disappointing showings in the Northeast and the rise of Alice Paul's National Woman's Party, made it time to pivot and seek a federal amendment.

THE WINNING PLAN

Only five years after the defeats of 1915, women throughout the nation cast their ballots in the election of 1920. The parallel and competing efforts of both NAWSA and the National Woman's Party (the successor to the Congressional Union) during those tumultuous years were responsible. Though each organization regarded the other as obstructing progress, both contributed to victory. While most of the rest of this final phase of the suffrage story unfolded at the national level, Massachusetts activists continued to play leading roles.

THE NATIONAL WOMAN'S PARTY

During the spring of 1916, Alice Paul and Lucy Burns sought to harness the power of women who were enfranchised in the West. The two hoped to persuade western women to vote against all Democratic Party candidates, including suffrage supporters, unless that party supported a federal amendment. Burns led twenty-three Congressional Union envoys by train through western states to rally and organize women voters. The "Suffrage Special," as the expedition was called, left Washington, D.C., on April 9. Those on board included Agnes and Katharine Morey, a mother-daughter team from Massachusetts. Agnes Morey had organized auto tours in the 1915 Massachusetts referendum campaign, and her daughter had previously campaigned in Kansas.

At each stop, envoys invited enfranchised women to attend a convention in Chicago in June to organize a Woman's Party composed of women voters. (In 1917, members of the Woman's Party and the Congressional Union would merge to form the National Woman's Party (NWP). For convenience, the Congressional Union and the Woman's Party are hereafter referred to collectively as the NWP.) When the Suffrage Special returned to Washington thirty-eight days later, the envoys, joined by supporters, marched to the Capitol to demand passage of what they called the Susan B. Anthony Amendment. The following month, at the June convention, attendees resolved to use their best efforts to defeat President Wilson and all Democratic Party candidates for Congress.

Only about 5 percent of suffragists belonged to the NWP, but Paul's smaller organization had several advantages.[1] It was a top-down disciplined body. The NWP had ample funding. Alva Belmont had broken with NAWSA, and her financial contributions largely sustained the NWP.[2] It also attracted many young, well-educated (and often well-off) activists who admired Paul's aggressive style. They were impatient with the perceived "plodding" nature of NAWSA, which still functioned primarily as an umbrella organization for largely independent state affiliates. NAWSA included many patient and polite mothers, while the NWP was comprised of headstrong and militant daughters.[3]

NAWSA

NAWSA now challenged that view—it would remain polite but no longer patient. When Anna Howard Shaw announced in late 1915 that she would not seek reelection as NAWSA president, a movement developed to draft former president Carrie Chapman Catt. She agreed to serve, but on the condition that she choose her own board. She wanted capable organizers whose personal and economic circumstances permitted full-time focus on suffrage. NAWSA elected Catt at its convention in December 1915.

She moved quickly to stem the still ongoing and damaging accusations that suffragists were enemies of marriage and the home. Calling such accusations "gross slander," NAWSA passed a resolution: "We believe the home is the foundation of the State; we believe in the sanctity of the marriage relationship; and furthermore, we believe that the ballot in the hands of women will strengthen the power of the home, and sustain the dignity and sacredness of marriage."[4]

NAWSA also passed a resolution expressing "appreciation for President Wilson's action in declaring in favor of the principle of equal suffrage."[5] His support for the New Jersey state amendment had indicated a willingness to change his mind, even though he remained unwilling to back a federal amendment. Catt believed that applying constant but not critical pressure on the president would lead him to eventually support a federal amendment.

President Woodrow Wilson. *Courtesy of the Library of Congress.*

In the spring of 1916, Catt issued a report in which she assessed NAWSA's internal disagreements about its best future strategy. She noted that while a considerable number of members concentrated in the South were "dead set" against a federal amendment, many other members felt the time had come to work for suffrage by the federal route. Concluding that NAWSA's strategic differences had "produced a great muddle," she announced her determination to turn NAWSA from a wandering herd of camels into a "purposeful caravan."[6]

Catt herself had become convinced that campaigning for a federal amendment was practical and preferable to continued exclusive reliance on state campaigns. State referenda had failed in the Northeast and were inconceivable in the South. Pursuing a federal amendment would allow NAWSA to take advantage of the considerable voting clout of western women. Additionally, the northeastern referenda campaigns had demonstrated that those states' elected politicians were more favorably disposed to woman suffrage—and more susceptible to pressure—than ordinary voters. A federal amendment required Congress to propose and state legislatures to ratify, but the process bypassed ordinary voters.

Catt also knew she needed to make NAWSA relevant to the many young, energetic suffragists who supported a federal amendment and might defect to the NWP. She briefly wondered whether reconciliation was possible between NAWSA and the NWP, but Paul would abandon neither her independence nor her pledge to hold the governing party accountable. She remained committed to opposing all Democrats, even those who personally supported woman suffrage. Another area of tension was the NWP's decision to organize state affiliates across the nation. In reaction, Catt sought to bolster NAWSA's own state affiliates. When Agnes Morey, who now chaired the small Massachusetts affiliate of the NWP, learned that Catt was visiting the state, Morey wrote, "Mrs. Catt is here simply to kill us if she can, but we will die very hard."[7]

Despite their other differences, NAWSA and the NWP agreed on the longstanding separation of gender from race discrimination and the exclusion, or at least invisibility, of black women from the white suffrage movement. NAWSA maintained that any involvement with black women's organizations would harm its prospects with southern senators. Alice Paul maintained that her goal was woman suffrage only—to see to it that the franchise conditions for every state were the same for women and men. The clear message was that neither suffrage organization would object if southern states maintained white supremacy by disenfranchising new black women voters as they had black men.[8]

During the summer of 1916, NAWSA sought to persuade the Republican and Democratic presidential nominating conventions to support a federal suffrage amendment. Using a new, high-profile tactic, five thousand NAWSA supporters wearing yellow sashes marched into the Republican convention and, a week later, showed up in force at the Democratic convention. But neither party platform endorsed the federal amendment. The Republicans favored "the extension of the suffrage to women, but recognize[d] the right of each state to settle this question for itself," while the Democrats recommended the "extension of the franchise to the women of the country by the States upon the same terms as to men." That summer brought another defeat, as Iowa rejected a state constitutional amendment to enfranchise women.

These events led Catt to call an emergency NAWSA Convention in Atlantic City, New Jersey, from September 6 to 10, 1916. President Woodrow Wilson, running for reelection and eager for support from women voters in western states, came to address the delegates. He affirmed his commitment to woman suffrage but refused to endorse a federal amendment, commenting that he gets "a little impatient" with "the discussion of the channels and methods by which it is to prevail." To great cheers, Anna Howard Shaw retorted, "We have waited long enough....We want it now." When Catt addressed the delegates, she made a pointed reference to the historic battle for the Fifteenth Amendment. "The woman's hour has struck," she announced.[9]

Catt proposed a new multifaceted "Winning Plan" to NAWSA's executive council, composed of national officers and leaders of state associations. NAWSA and its state affiliates would lobby members of Congress to support a federal amendment. To do so effectively, NAWSA would revitalize its Congressional Committee, which had been dormant since Paul and Burns had been removed as chairs. NAWSA would remain nonpartisan and continue to judge each candidate's individual attitude and record.

State organizations were assigned additional tasks. Those in full suffrage states would seek resolutions from their state legislatures supporting a federal amendment. Other state affiliates would seek partial suffrage legislation permitting women to vote in presidential elections. Going forward, campaigns for state constitutional amendments would be restricted to states where success was likely. This last restriction would save resources and avoid the adverse publicity and decreased morale that accompanied state defeats. Last, NAWSA and its affiliates were not to become distracted by divisive, ancillary issues such as the prohibition of alcohol.

Catt told the executive council that the Winning Plan must be kept secret because suffrage opponents would not be prepared for battle on so many fronts. She obtained a commitment from more than thirty-six state associations to support her plan. "From that moment," she later wrote, "there were no defections, no doubts, no differences in [NAWSA]. A great army in perfect discipline moved forward to its goal."[10] Maud Wood Park was exhilarated. She felt "like Moses on the mountain top after the Promised Land had been shown to him and he knew the long years of wandering in the Wilderness were over."[11] Southern delegates were dismayed, however. Fearing that a federal amendment would call attention to the South's odious, systematic disenfranchisement of black voters, they claimed that "states' rights" were at stake.

LOBBYISTS, PICKETS, AND WAR

Catt placed Maud Wood Park in charge of congressional lobbying efforts, and she was later named chair of NAWSA's Congressional Committee. She began her new responsibilities soon after the election of 1916 had returned Wilson to the White House. That election also marked the election of the first congresswoman, Jeanette Rankin, a Republican from Montana.

Park's immediate goals were threefold. She sought to persuade the Senate to vote on a federal amendment following an expected favorable report from the Committee on Woman Suffrage. She also sought to persuade the House Judiciary Committee to report on the woman suffrage amendment, even if the report was unfavorable, so that the House, too, would vote. She additionally hoped to convince the House to establish a committee on the rights of women.

In her posthumously published memoir of her congressional work, *Front Door Lobby*, Park explained that "Front Door Lobby was the half-humorous, half-kindly name" a reporter gave NAWSA's Congressional Committee. But she made clear that the Congressional Committee, which operated in meticulous secrecy, did not eschew "backdoor" methods. She coordinated lobbying efforts out of "Suffrage House," a rundown mansion with sixteen bedrooms in Washington, D.C. Park had a small political staff, which was supplemented by a large cadre of well-connected women able to finance their own trips to Washington. Her closest partner was Helen Hamilton Gardener, a writer who served as NAWSA's chief liaison to President Wilson's administration.

Park and her associates collected detailed information about each senator and representative, including their family, interests, and positions on other issues. She promulgated "lobby rules" containing a long series of "don'ts" for the many visiting suffragists who paid personal visits to senators and representatives from their home states. These included: "don't nag; don't boast; don't threaten; don't lose your temper [no matter the provocation]; don't stay too long; don't talk about your work where you can be overheard; don't give the member interviewed an opportunity to declare himself against the amendment; don't do anything to close the door to the next advocate of suffrage." Park knew firsthand the challenges of maintaining one's temper in the face of provocation. When she met with Massachusetts Republican senator Henry Cabot Lodge, an avowed anti-suffragist, he "snarled, 'I know why you want a federal amendment....It's because you realize that you'll never get another state by popular vote.'"[12]

As Park labored in Washington, Catt made plans for a generous bequest from the estate of Frank Leslie, the widow of publisher Frank Leslie. (Miriam Leslie had changed her name to Frank following her husband's death.) She had revived her husband's publishing business and left her nearly $2 million estate to Catt in 1914 "to the furtherance of the cause of Woman's Suffrage," but challenges by displeased relatives consumed two years and half the bequest in legal fees and settlements. Given that

NAWSA's entire annual budget was $100,000, Leslie's bequest nevertheless offered enormous potential.

Catt established the Leslie Woman Suffrage Commission in New York City with a staff of twenty-five to prepare and disseminate pro-suffrage news throughout the nation. She also purchased the *Woman's Journal* for $50,000. Despite its extraordinary influence, the publication only had thirty thousand paid subscribers, leading to ongoing financial struggles. Catt moved the *Woman's Journal* to Madison Avenue, renamed it the *Woman Citizen* and pronounced it NAWSA's "official organ."[13] (Following convention, it will continue to be referred to as the *Woman's Journal*.) NAWSA press secretary Rose Young became editor-in-chief, and Alice Stone Blackwell was named special contributing editor. In the first NAWSA issue, published on June 2, 1917, Catt paid tribute to Stone Blackwell and her parents. She wrote that the *Woman's Journal* "has been history maker and history recorder....The suffrage success of today is not conceivable without the *Woman's Journal's* part in it."[14]

Park's lobbying effort confronted two new and complex challenges in 1917: NWP's picketing the White House and the nation's entry into World War I. Picketing was another high-profile tactic Alice Paul adopted from British suffragettes. The NWP decided to post pickets to demonstrate its dissatisfaction with Wilson's failure to support a federal amendment. Paul and Burns may have also found it necessary to embrace a fresh tactic after their election strategy had failed. In 1916, Wilson had won all but one state where women were enfranchised. Other issues, such as the war in Europe, had weighed more heavily on voters' minds.

The first group of twelve "Silent Sentinels" stood in front of the White House on January 10, 1917, and nearly daily thereafter. Their banners asked Wilson, "What will you do for Woman Suffrage?" and "How long must women wait for their liberty?"

Park reported that the Silent Sentinels made her congressional work harder, as many politicians and their constituents objected to women conducting public protests, particularly outside the White House. When Park explained that NAWSA did not endorse the pickets, she was often told, "You can't expect us to vote for you if you can't agree among yourselves." She pointed out that men within the same party were not without their differences but noted wryly that "sauce for the gander was rarely accepted as sauce for the goose."[15]

Although Wilson had campaigned on a promise to keep the United States out of war, the nation entered World War I on April 6, 1917. Catt was

NWP pickets at the White House, February 1917. *Courtesy of the Library of Congress.*

an avowed pacifist, as were a number of other prominent suffragists. But despite her personal opposition to American intervention in a European war, she was convinced that NAWSA leaders must work "doubly hard" to support both the war effort and suffrage. Women's devoted service during a war waged to "keep the world safe for democracy" would, Catt believed, hasten passage of the suffrage amendment. This had happened with black men, whose Civil War military service was a key factor in the passage of the Fifteenth Amendment.

When war became imminent, NAWSA's Executive Council issued a public declaration to President Wilson and Congress, stating, "With no intention of laying aside our constructive forward work to secure the vote [for women]… we offer our services…and in so far as we are authorized, we pledge the loyal support of our more than two million members."[16] When war began, Catt served on the Women's Committee of the Council of National Defense and the Women's Division of the Liberty Loan Committee. Shaw led the Woman's Committee of the Council of National Defense. Other NAWSA leaders also assumed leadership positions. MWSA, like many state associations, replaced its annual suffrage festival with a patriotic bazaar to raise funds for war relief, and many state leaders joined the Massachusetts Division of the Woman's Committee of the Council of National Defense.[17]

Catt was also determined to keep suffrage in the forefront. "Woman suffrage," she wrote in the *Woman's Journal*, "is a part of this great world struggle; for there can be no real democracy which leaves women out." Park quietly continued her lobbying efforts, although Wilson and congressional leaders had made it clear that only war measures would be considered. This "complicated and retarded the work for the federal suffrage amendment," reported Park, but "some progress" was made.[18]

The NWP took a different approach when war began. Paul refused to support the war or to halt picketing, although the English suffragettes had suspended their suffrage campaign when war began in Europe in 1914. Paul believed the American women's rights movement had made a strategic error during the Civil War when it suspended its activism in support of women, and she was determined to do differently. The NWP wanted to send a clear message to politicians and the public that they were not going to cease their campaign until they won the vote. The pickets stationed in front of the White House now carried banners addressing the president as "Kaiser Wilson" and mocking his pledge that the United States was fighting "for the right of those who submit to authority to have a voice in their government." In June 1917, when a Russian delegation was scheduled to meet with Wilson, pickets held a banner that declared, "We, the women of America, tell you that America is not a democracy."

These banners led to massive criticism, including by NAWSA. Catt criticized the protests as "absurd [and] ill-timed" and urged the press and public to ignore "the tactics of the isolated handful" of protestors. She reminded the public that NAWSA's labors were responsible for every grant of suffrage across the nation and that its law-abiding and nonpartisan methods were "constructive, forward-looking, and forward-leaping."[19]

The NWP's efforts remained in the public eye, however. Attention grew when the police made their first arrests on June 22, 1917, charging Lucy Burns and Katharine Morey with blocking sidewalk traffic. By the end of June, six NWP pickets had been sentenced to three days in jail. Picketing and arrests continued throughout the summer and fall of 1917. Ultimately, 500 protestors were arrested and 168 jailed, most in the notorious Occoquan Workhouse in Virginia. In October, Paul was sentenced to serve seven months. Relying on the technique she had used in England, she argued that she was not subject to laws that she had no role in making and demanded to be treated as a political prisoner. When officials rejected her demand, she began a hunger strike. Prison officials responded by force-feeding Paul. Burns and fifteen other prisoners also began hunger strikes following a "Night of

Terror" (November 15, 1917), when prison officials beat Burns and many other incarcerated NWP pickets.

Although much of the public had initially been unsympathetic to the protestors, their harsh treatment produced an outcry. It grew louder when Paul was moved into a psychiatric prison ward. And it grew louder still when the public saw photos of thirty haggard and exhausted suffragists when they appeared in court later in November. Attorney Dudley Field Malone, the collector of the Port of New York, resigned to provide free legal services to the suffragists. He sought habeas corpus relief from what he alleged was unlawful imprisonment. Several days later, all of the imprisoned suffragists were released.

Katharine Morey. *Courtesy of the Library of Congress.*

NAWSA, meanwhile, had made great strides in implementing Catt's Winning Plan. Park's lobbying efforts had led the House to appoint a Committee on Woman Suffrage in September 1917. The day after Paul began her hunger strike, the East Coast's sea wall blocking the suffrage tide was breached when New York voters approved a constitutional amendment enfranchising women.[20] (Unlike Massachusetts, New York had made another attempt following the 1915 defeat. New York state suffrage leaders and Catt, who had led that state's 1915 effort, had correctly judged that a new campaign that included a heavy emphasis on door-to-door canvassing stood a good chance of success.)

The New York victory placed members of the nation's largest congressional delegation on notice that failure to support a federal amendment might provoke voters' wrath. Suffrage supporters could also now argue the extreme illogic of women being able to vote in New York but not in, for example, the contiguous states of Connecticut, New Jersey, Massachusetts, Pennsylvania, and Vermont. Additional momentum was gained when Oklahoma and South Dakota enfranchised women and five states, including Rhode Island, granted women presidential suffrage.[21]

Another barrier fell at the end of 1917. Congress enacted a prohibition amendment (the Eighteenth Amendment) on December 18, and it was

NWP protesting treatment of arrested pickets, 1917. *Courtesy of the Library of Congress.*

ratified thirteen months later. The prohibition movement had received new momentum when war began. Congress enacted a wartime prohibition act to conserve grain for the army and civilian population. Plus, many breweries were owned by German immigrants, and closing them was considered "patriotic." The women's movement was an unintended beneficiary of the prohibition amendment. Its adoption marked the end of the liquor industry's relentless lobbying against woman suffrage.

At NAWSA's convention in December 1917, Catt observed that American democratic principles are the slogan of "every movement toward political liberty the world round" and argued that American aspirations for global leadership required woman suffrage. The *Woman's Journal* ran an eye-catching notice listing the many ways in which women were supporting the war effort. They served as mechanics, nurses, doctors, army cooks, and ambulance drivers. They filled men's positions in industry and trade and on farms. In exchange for this extensive and varied service, women asked for one thing only: enfranchisement.[22]

As 1918 began, NAWSA pledged to use its clout against suffrage opponents in Congress, and this time, representatives and senators facing reelection took note. For his part, President Wilson was eager to put this source of domestic divisiveness behind him and assert America's commitment to democratic

Women Farmerettes during World War I. *Courtesy of the Library of Congress.*

Ordnance plant in Cambridge during World War I. *Courtesy of the Library of Congress.*

principles on the world stage. Additionally, the war had propelled woman suffrage forward in other nations. In March 1917, when revolutionaries deposed the Russian czar, women had gained full suffrage. Many European nations would soon follow.

On January 9, 1918, President Wilson announced his support for a federal amendment enfranchising women. It was, he said, a war measure, and an "act of right and justice to the women of the country and the world."[23] The following day, Congresswoman Jeanette Rankin introduced the Nineteenth Amendment on the floor of the House of Representatives.

On January 10, 1918, the House passed the amendment, 274–136, just clearing the two-thirds hurdle. In all, 164 Republicans and 103 Democrats supported the amendment (as did seven members of other parties); 34 Republicans and 101 Democrats comprised the opposition. Nearly a quarter of all Republican opponents were from Massachusetts, where only 3 of 11 Republican congressmen supported the amendment. Even at this late stage, the state's Republicans continued to have a faction of blueblood

"The Weaker Sex?" Kenneth Russell Chamberlain, *Puck*, November 7, 1914. *Courtesy of the Library of Congress.*

conservatives out of step with their national party. Democrats who opposed the amendment were concentrated in the South.

NAWSA and the NWP each claimed credit for the House vote. Catt dismissed the notion that the NWP had helped the cause, stating, "You may assure any who make that claim that it was accomplished in spite of them."[24] Paul maintained that her organization had prodded Wilson and House Democrats to act to save their seats in the next elections. In truth, both deserve credit. NAWSA had laid the organizational groundwork for decades and executed Catt's Winning Plan. It was an effective political machine that claimed two million members and had earned politicians' respect. The NWP's protests—and the resulting imprisonments—had captured the public's attention and aroused their sympathy. The NWP's militant methods also led Wilson to find common ground with the more moderate NAWSA. It might be most accurate to say that NAWSA laid the tracks and drove the train, but the NWP had pushed the throttle.

All eyes turned to the Senate, which proved more intractable than the House. Throughout the muggy Washington summer of 1918, the

NWP continued to post pickets and NAWSA continued to lobby. The NWP believed that its pickets kept pressure on President Wilson. Park complained that the pickets "probably cost [the amendment] three votes." She admitted to Robert Hunter, her husband, that the "nervous wear and tear" of seeking enough Senate votes had made her "harassed and depressed and irritable."[25]

Ultimately, in a dramatic gesture of support, President Wilson appeared before the Senate on September 30, 1918, to urge passage of the amendment. He stated, "We have made partners of women during this war" and called passage of the amendment "vitally essential" to the United States' ability to lead the world to democracy.[26] Wilson's decision to appear before the Senate was presumably a political calculation. He wanted to make sure that he and the Democratic Party would receive credit (and not face a backlash) from woman voters in the November midterm election, despite more Republicans than Democrats supporting a federal amendment.

When the Senate voted the next day, the amendment fell two votes short of the necessary two-thirds. Though Republicans had voted nearly three to one in favor, both Republican senators from Massachusetts, John Weeks and Henry Cabot Lodge, voted no. NAWSA responded by targeting four senators, including Senator Weeks, for defeat in November. (Lodge would not be facing reelection that year.) Weeks's challenger was Democrat David Walsh, a former governor and suffrage supporter. Massachusetts had not elected a Democratic senator for over a century.

MWSA, meanwhile, had not been idle after the defeat in 1915. Volunteers had continued to give speeches, canvass voters, lobby state and federal legislators, and generate a steady stream of pro-suffrage literature.[27] Alice Stone Blackwell and Teresa Crowley were among the leaders who promptly formed a nonpartisan Anti-Weeks Campaign Committee. To demonstrate their outreach to diverse constituencies, the steering committee included representatives from the Catholic, Jewish, and trade union communities. The NWP, which continued to target Democrats for defeat, was not involved in this effort.

The campaign against Weeks unfolded in difficult times. An influenza pandemic had begun in late August when several sailors became ill on military ships in Boston Harbor. By October 1, 1918, 85,000 influenza cases had been reported in Massachusetts, leading to about 200 flu-related deaths each day. Nationally, a staggering 25 million would become ill, and 675,000 would die. In addition, war continued in Europe, although Germany would sign an armistice agreement with the Allies on November 11, 1918.

Relying on the tactics polished in past campaigns, Crowley traveled to Washington to research Weeks's voting record. Members of the anti-Weeks committee mailed leaflets to registered Republicans detailing his opposition to progressive measures intended to benefit soldiers, sailors, farmers, wage-earners, and others. MWSA placed ads with the heading "Senator Weeks's Record: It Speaks for Itself" in Republican newspapers.[28]

The committee wrote to thirty-five thousand women known to support suffrage, asking each to use her influence to obtain at least one anti-Weeks vote. Women labor union representatives toured the state. Jewish and Catholic supporters campaigned in cities. Men of the Equal Suffrage League placed their names on large newspaper advertisements. All of these efforts combined in a victorious effort. On Election Day, Walsh defeated Weeks by twenty thousand votes. In addition to eliminating an anti-suffrage vote, this success in Massachusetts "put the fear of the Lord into the hearts of every politician," said Luscomb.[29]

The results of the 1918 election placed Republicans in control of the House and Senate. Catt wrote in the *Woman's Journal* that NAWSA was committed to achieving full suffrage for every American woman before the next federal election in 1920. In a jab at the NWP, she also stressed the success of NAWSA's methods of appealing to logic and justice and its avoidance of militant and unconstitutional methods.[30]

Within days of the November 1918 election, the armistice marking the end of World War I was signed. In an effort to pressure Wilson to secure Senate support, Agnes Morey and other members of the NWP burned copies of his speeches in Lafayette Park, across the street from the White House. Catt believed the NWP's "shocking and outrageous" methods made the remaining work harder.[31] But NAWSA, too, was determined to pressure Wilson to move quickly.

The lame-duck Senate voted on the Nineteenth Amendment on February 10, 1919, but fell one vote short. Time was now of the essence. The lame-duck Congress was due to adjourn on March 4, and the new Congress was not scheduled to convene until December. If the Senate did not pass the amendment before adjourning, both NAWSA and the NWP intended to pressure Wilson to call a special spring session of the new Congress.

President Wilson was in Europe working on the postwar peace accords until February. When he returned to the United States, his ship was scheduled to dock in Boston. The NWP decided to greet him with a protest. On February 24, 1919, twenty-two NWP members stood in front of the Massachusetts State House with banners imploring Wilson to secure the one vote needed to pass the suffrage amendment. The protestors were largely from Massachusetts; sixteen, including Katharine Morey, were from greater Boston.[32]

The Boston police arrested the protestors before the president arrived and charged them with loitering. It was a "most extraordinary thing," complained Agnes Morey, "to arrest only those who loitered for liberty." A judge fined each arrested woman five dollars and, when they refused to pay, ordered them detained in the Charles Street jail for eight days. Katharine Morey was among those released—over their objections—when an unknown man paid the fines. Her mother speculated that this mystery man was fictitious and that authorities were eager to release these high-profile prisoners. These were the final women jailed for seeking the ballot.[33]

In contrast to the NWP's greeting, NAWSA gave Wilson flowers and thanked him for his efforts on behalf of the Nineteenth Amendment. But keeping the political pressure on, Catt pointedly reminded Wilson and Congress that twelve million women were already enfranchised and would be casting their votes in the next election.[34]

Many pro-suffrage congressmen and senators also urged Wilson to act. He hardly needed additional prompting. Great Britain and Canada had enfranchised most women in 1918, as had Germany, Austria, Poland, Latvia, and Estonia. Moreover, 1919 was shaping up to be a tumultuous year domestically. Fears of communists and anarchists dominated the news. Labor strikes were widespread.

Seeking to put an end to one divisive issue, Wilson called the new Congress into session on May 19, 1919. Because this was a new Congress, the House needed to pass the suffrage amendment again. It did so on May 21 by a vote of 304–89. This time, 8 of 15 Massachusetts congressmen favored the amendment, including 6 of 11 Republicans.

Opponents in the Senate sought to delay a vote. Senator Henry Cabot Lodge argued that Senate action was inappropriate because it would override the will of the people as reflected in the referenda results in those states that had defeated woman suffrage. Notwithstanding these efforts, on June 4, 1919, the U.S. Senate passed the proposed amendment fifty-six to twenty-five, with fifteen senators not voting. Walsh supported the amendment, while Lodge opposed it. Southern Democrats cast the large majority of nay votes.

Catt "tendered [NAWSA's] abiding gratitude" to its friends of suffrage in both parties. She and Park attended the signing ceremony at the Capitol and headed the receiving line at NAWSA's celebration.

There was little time to celebrate, however. Both NAWSA and the NWP immediately announced they would campaign for ratification by the necessary thirty-six states at a pace that would enable women to vote in 1920. Catt asked Park to lead the ratification efforts in New England, but she declined, preferring to be free to campaign throughout the nation.

Teresa Crowley and Gertrude Halladay Leonard led the Massachusetts ratification campaign. Their first task was to ensure that the state legislative committee assigned to report on the Nineteenth Amendment acted quickly and favorably. Concerned that chair Henry Achin of Lowell might oppose the amendment, Luscomb took charge of a squad of volunteers who gathered signatures on a pro-suffrage petition. When it was delivered to Achin, the number and caliber of the signatures left him "poring over the petitions with his eyes almost bugging out," she recalled. His committee voted favorably.[35]

That first step was followed by a legislative hearing attended by nearly five hundred women. Alice Stone Blackwell, Margaret Foley, and Katharine Morey were among the many women and men who spoke in support of ratification. Opponents claimed one last time that there was no proof that public opinion had changed since the defeat of woman suffrage in 1915 and that "forcing" suffrage upon women defied "every principle of free government."[36]

This time, their efforts were in vain. On June 25, 1919, Massachusetts became the eighth state to ratify the Nineteenth Amendment. The state Senate supported the amendment 34–5, and the House, 185–47. Alice Stone Blackwell wrote that while each state's ratification brought joy, none "aroused more rejoicing among suffragists than the victory in Massachusetts—rock-ribbed old Massachusetts, birthplace of Lucy Stone and Susan B. Anthony, battleground of this cause from its earliest years and also the home for almost a generation of the oldest and strongest anti-suffrage association."[37]

By February 1920, twenty-seven states had ratified the Nineteenth Amendment. NAWSA held a "Victory Convention" to demand prompt ratification by the remaining states. It also prepared for the next phase of its history. The League of Women Voters was formally organized as the successor to NAWSA. Maud Wood Park was elected the first national president of the nonpartisan league, and Catt became the honorary president.

By August 1920, thirty-five states had ratified the amendment; eight states had rejected it (Alabama, Delaware, Georgia, Louisiana, Maryland, Mississippi, South Carolina and Virginia); and five had not yet voted (Connecticut, Florida, North Carolina, Tennessee and Vermont). The governors of Connecticut and Vermont refused to call their legislatures into

"The sky is now her limit," Elmer Andrews Bushnell, *Current History*, October 1920. *Courtesy of the Library of Congress.*

special sessions, and defeats were anticipated in North Carolina and Florida. All eyes turned to the closely divided state of Tennessee.

Pro- and anti-suffragists came out in force for what journalists called the war of the yellow versus red roses. The Tennessee Senate approved the amendment, but the House vote was tied. In a revote, Harry Burn, a twenty-four-year-old Republican wearing a red rose, broke the tie and supported

National League of Women Voters Board of Directors at the Chicago Convention in 1920, including Park *(front left)* and Catt *(front right)*. *Courtesy of the Library of Congress.*

ratification. His mother had sent instructions: "vote for suffrage, and don't keep them in doubt....Don't forget to be a good boy."

On August 26, 1920, the U.S. Secretary of State issued a proclamation officially making the Nineteenth Amendment a part of the U.S. Constitution. The amendment provides:

Section 1. The right of citizens of the United States to vote shall not be denied or abridged by the United States or by any state on account of sex.

Section 2. Congress shall have power to enforce this article by appropriate legislation.

The many decades of struggle were finally over. Carrie Chapman Catt, Maud Wood Park, and Helen Gardener met with President Wilson at the White House. Alice Paul, who was not invited, unfurled a banner with thirty-six victory stars at the NWP headquarters. In Boston, church bells rang as hundreds of women singing a suffrage hymn marched from Boston Common to Faneuil Hall.[38]

Massachusetts suffragists held a victory parade and dinner the following month. Alice Stone Blackwell and Maud Wood Park both addressed celebrants. Stone Blackwell urged women to use their "great power" to "the best advantage." Park told her "fellow citizens" that "we owe it to the women who have made today possible to be worth being enfranchised." Though they had earned the right to bask in the aftermath of their triumph, Stone Blackwell and Park had other plans. True to character, they immediately moved onward. Stone Blackwell urged women who were fortunate enough to be part of the suffrage movement in the years of its success to "become the pioneers of the unpopular social movements of today." Park commenced an educational lecture tour to prepare women to exercise their new right on November 2, 1920.[39]

CONCLUSION

Adoption of the Nineteenth Amendment was the end of only one story. Much work remained. The amendment did not secure the vote to women (and men) disenfranchised because of race. It did not lead to the abolition of other laws that perpetuated gender discrimination. In many states, including Massachusetts, it was read so narrowly that it did not even invalidate laws limiting jury service to men. Nor did women become a unified voting bloc dedicated to obtaining additional legal rights for themselves or other victims of historical injustice. Indeed, activists within NAWSA (now reconstituted as the League of Women Voters) and the NWP remained at odds even after 1920. The former supported protective legislation that would improve conditions for laboring women and children, while the latter favored strict legal equality. Nevertheless, despite its limitations, the Nineteenth Amendment transformed and democratized the nation. It enabled American women to enter all future battles armed with the ballot—the most valuable weapon in a democratic society.

Massachusetts suffragists performed both starring and supportive roles throughout the long campaign. Lucy Stone, in particular, was a trailblazer in the nineteenth century. She was the most prominent spokesperson for women's rights in the antebellum era and a leader of the first-ever national woman's rights convention and its successors. After the Civil War, she rejected appeals to racism and defended the Fifteenth Amendment. She formed the American Woman Suffrage Association, which undertook the grueling, frustrating, but absolutely essential work of building state organizations and supporting state campaigns. She began and led the newspaper that was vital to the entire movement. Throughout, she worked with a committed group of allies, many of whom also had roots in the abolitionist movement.

Stone's daughter continued her mother's work. Alice Stone Blackwell sustained and expanded the *Woman's Journal*, which linked suffragists across the nation. She recognized the importance of uniting the divided suffrage movement and was instrumental in the creation of NAWSA. She helped the state's suffrage movement weather the dark days at the end of the nineteenth century. A devoted daughter, she also wrote a biography of her mother, but this effort arrived in 1930, long after Anthony and Stanton had cemented their legacy.

In the twentieth century, Maud Wood Park and other young women joined Alice Stone Blackwell in the Massachusetts suffrage movement. Buoyed by Carrie Chapman Catt's leadership of NAWSA, members of the state's new generation organized college students and wage-earning women, allied with the labor movement, and adopted innovative campaign tactics. Even though they were unable to secure the vote for the women of Massachusetts, many of their efforts were influential far beyond the state's borders. When NAWSA shifted its focus to a federal amendment, Park became the lead lobbyist in Washington. Her state allies were finally able to win an important local victory; they unseated an anti-suffrage U.S. senator at a crucial moment.

Of course, other states also had vital roles in the long suffrage story. The first victories were in the West. New York was another center of the movement, and its successful 1917 campaign provided the national campaign with critical momentum. But Massachusetts' role has been particularly overlooked. One reason was the post–Civil War schism and the resulting one-sided history written by Anthony and Stanton that has influenced public perceptions ever since. Another reason is that Massachusetts never enfranchised its own women and has not, therefore, received the attention paid to states that waged successful, decisive campaigns (e.g., Wyoming, Colorado, California, and New York). Massachusetts has typically been regarded as a story of failure rather than one of achievement balanced by failure. This book is an effort to present a more complete picture.

While this book focuses on the past rather than the present, it also has relevance to our own times. Against long odds, suffrage advocates waged a persistent battle for equal rights that involved many thousands of women and lasted nearly a century. Their example reminds us to never relinquish hope or concede defeat in our efforts to make the world more just.

Notes

I relied heavily on primary sources for my research. Due to space constraints, the endnotes below identify only the title of primary source documents that are available online. An online version of the notes, available at www.WomanSuffrageMA.com, identifies the URL or the online library. I made particular use of two superb online libraries: Alexander Street's *Women and Social Movements in the United States, 1600–2000* and Gale Primary Sources' *Nineteenth Century Collections*. The version below lists only the dates for newspaper articles; the online version also includes the article titles so that interested readers may more easily locate them. Reports of votes in the U.S. Congress are from govtrack.us/congress.

The online version of the endnotes also includes expanded discussions of numerous points I make in the text.

A bibliography is available at www.WomanSuffrageMA.com.

Abbreviations used in notes:
Globe: *Boston Globe*
HWS: *History of Woman Suffrage*
NYT: *New York Times*
WJ: *Woman's Journal*
WRC-SL: Women's Rights Collection, Schlesinger Library, Radcliffe Institute, Harvard University
SSC-SC: Sophia Smith Collection of Women's History, Smith College

Introduction

1. I use the term *woman suffrage* rather than women's suffrage because that is how the participants referred to their movement. A *suffragist* advocated extending the franchise to women. A *suffragette* was a militant British suffragist; suffragettes adopted this moniker after critics used it to mock them. A suffrage opponent was known as a *remonstrant* or *anti-suffragist*. Suffragists referred to *sex discrimination*, and I will generally use that term rather than *gender discrimination*.
2. Angelina Grimke, Letter XII to Catharine Beecher.
3. Kathryn Kish Sklar, *Women's Rights Emerges within the Antislavery Movement* (Boston; New York: Bedford/St. Martin's 2000), 160.

Chapter 1

1. Sklar, *Women's Rights*, 117 (Angelina Grimké to Jane Smith, July 25, 1837).
2. In a letter dated March 31, 1776, Abigail Adams famously urged her husband, John Adams, to "remember the ladies" in the Code of Laws he and other Patriots would write for the new nation. Although her letter did not launch a movement, it has and continues to inspire women.
3. Barbara F. Berenson, *Boston and the Civil War: Hub of the Second Revolution* (Charleston, SC: The History Press 2014), 31.
4. Mark Perry, ed., *Sarah Grimké and Angelina Grimké: On Slavery and Abolitionism, Essays and Letters* (New York: Penguin, 2015), 123.
5. Maria Stewart, one known exception, is discussed below. In 1828, Frances Wright, a radical Scottish-born utopianist, became the first woman to publicly lecture in the United States.
6. Proceedings, Anti-Slavery Convention of American Women, May 1837.
7. Sklar, *Women's Rights*, 110–12 (Angelina Grimké to Jane Smith, May 29, 1837).
8. Ibid., 112–14 (Maria Chapman to New England Anti-Slavery Societies, June 7, 1837).
9. Ibid., 115–16 (Angelina Grimké to Jane Smith, June 1837).
10. Pastoral Letter of the General Association of Congregational Ministers of Massachusetts, June 27, 1837.
11. Berenson, *Boston and the Civil War*, 98.
12. Sklar, *Women's Rights*, 108 (Catharine Beecher, "Essay on Slavery and Abolitionism, with Reference to the Duty of American Females," 1837).

13. Sarah Grimké, Letters on the Equality of the Sexes and the Condition of Women, Addressed to Mary S. Parker, President of the Boston Female Anti-Slavery Society.

14. Angelina Grimké, Letters to Catharine E. Beecher, in reply to "An Essay of Slavery and Abolitionism."

15. Gilbert H. Barnes, and Dwight L. Dumond, *Letters of Weld, Grimke, and Grimke, 1822–1844* (Washington, D.C.: American Historical Association, 1934), 425–32.

16. Ibid.

17. Perry, *Sarah Grimké and Angelina Grimké*, 329–31.

18. Angelina Grimké, Speech at Pennsylvania Hall.

19. Sklar, *Women's Rights*, 160–61 (Angelina Grimké to Anne Warren Weston, July 15, 1838).

Chapter 2

1. Dorothy Sterling, *Ahead of Her Time: Abby Kelley and the Politics of Antislavery* (New York: Norton, 1991), 53–54.

2. Ibid., 231.

3. Sally G. McMillen, *Lucy Stone: An Unapologetic Life* (New York: Oxford University Press, 2015), 65.

4. Samuel J. May, *The Rights and Condition of Women* (1845).

5. Andrea Moore Kerr, *Lucy Stone: Speaking Out for Equality* (New Brunswick, NJ: Rutgers University Press, 1992), 48, 196.

6. Lucy Stone Papers, Folder 1053, WRC-SL.

7. Kerr, *Lucy Stone*, 52.

8. Sklar, *Women's Rights*, 169.

9. As will be discussed in chapter 4, contemporaneous evidence shows that the claim that Mott and Stanton had developed the idea for a women's rights convention when they met in London in 1840 was created years later.

10. See Lawrence Friedman, *History of American Law*, 3rd ed. (New York: Simon & Schuster, 2005), 146.

11. Methodist preachers were among the leaders of the Great Awakening.

12. Report of the Woman's Rights Convention Held at Seneca Falls, July 1848.

13. Frederick Douglass, remarks in *North Star*.

14. Lisa Tetrault, *The Myth of Seneca Falls: Memory and the Women's Suffrage Movement, 1848–1898* (Chapel Hill: University North Carolina, 2014), 13.

15. A recent local convention in Salem, Ohio, may also have contributed to the decision to plan a national convention.

16. McMillen, *Lucy Stone*, 90.

17. Wherever possible, I have relied on the *Proceedings of the Woman's Rights Convention, Held at Worcester, October 23 and 24, 1850*. I have supplemented the official *Proceedings* with newspaper reports that include summaries of speeches not included in the *Proceedings*, including those of Sojourner Truth and Ernestine Rose. For those, I relied on John F. McClymer, *This High and Holy Moment: The First National Woman's Rights Convention, Worcester, 1850* (New York: Harcourt Brace, 1999), 140, 143–44, 148–51 and the website of the Worcester Women's History Project.

18. Sojourner Truth, *Ain't I a Woman*. There are differing accounts of her remarks.

19. See MassMoments, First National Woman's Rights Convention Ends in Worcester, October 24, 1840.

20. *Proceedings of the Woman's Rights Convention, Held at Worcester, October 15 and 16, 1851*.

21. McMillen, *Lucy Stone*, 79

22. The primary motivation for the convention was a desire by some to reconsider how legislators were apportioned among cities and towns.

23. McMillen, *Lucy Stone*, 97–98; McClymer, *High and Holy Moment*, 180–83.

24. Ibid., 109–10.

25. Lucy Stone's letter to the Tax Collector, December 18, 1858.

26. McMillen, *Lucy Stone*, 111.

27. *HWS*, 721–22; Kerr, *Lucy Stone*, 111–12.

Chapter 3

1. Berenson, *Boston and the Civil War*, 98

2. Proceedings of the National Convention of Colored Men, Held in Syracuse, October 4–7, 1864.

3. Meeting of the Massachusetts Anti-Slavery Society, May 1865.

4. Ibid.

5. That section would also prohibit the states from abridging the privileges or immunities of citizens; depriving any person of life, liberty or property without due process of law; and denying any person the equal protection of the laws.

6. Petition for Universal Suffrage, January 29, 1866.

7. Proceedings of the Eleventh National Woman's Rights Convention, New York, May 10, 1866.

8. Frances Ellen Watkins Harper, *We Are All Bound Up Together*, 1866.

9. Patricia G. Holland, "George Francis Train and the Woman Suffrage Movement, 1867–70," *Books at Iowa* 46 (1987): 8.

10. *New York Herald*, December 15, 1867; Faye E. Dudden, *Fighting Chance: The Struggle over Woman Suffrage and Black Suffrage in Reconstruction America* (New York: Oxford University Press, 2011), 140–45.

11. *Revolution*, January 8, 1868.

12. Dudden, *Fighting Chance*, 86, 104–7.

13. Ibid., 45, 150.

14. Henry Blackwell, *What the South Can Do*; McMillen, *Lucy Stone*, 166.

15. *Revolution*, July 9, 1868; October 1, 1868.

16. The Boston Woman's Rights Convention, January 1869.

17. *Revolution*, December 24, 1868; February 4, 1869.

18. Dudden, *Fighting Chance*, 3. See also Alice F. Berenson, "Torn Asunder: The Woman Suffrage Movement Divides Over the Primacy of Black or Woman Suffrage," unpublished manuscript, 2011.

19. II *HWS* 379–83.

20. Ibid., 383–84.

21. Dudden, *Fighting Chance*, 180.

22. Nell Painter, *Sojourner Truth: A Life, A Symbol* (New York: W.W. Norton, 1996), 232. Truth participated, however, in NWSA's 1872 voting campaign.

23. Constitution of the American Woman Suffrage Association.

24. *WJ*, January 8, 1870.

25. Ibid., January 8, 1870; January 7, 1871.

26. Ibid., January 7, 1871.

Chapter 4

1. George Hoar, *Woman Suffrage: Essential to the True Republic* (Boston: American Woman Suffrage Association, 1873).

2. Barbara Weltner, "The Cult of True Womanhood: 1820–1860" *American Quarterly* (1966): 151.

3. *Bradwell v. State of Illinois*, 83 U.S. 130 (1872).

4. Stephen Jay Gould, *The Panda's Thumb*. (New York: W.W. Norton, 1980), 152.

5. Paul Quigley, "The Birth of Thanksgiving," *New York Times*, November 28, 2013.

6. Victoria Woodhull, Speech in Steinway Hall, November 20, 1871.

7. Andrea Kerr, "White Women's Rights, Black Men's Wrongs," in Marjorie Spruill Wheeler, *One Woman, One Vote: Rediscovering the Woman Suffrage Movement* (Troutdale, OR: NewSage Press, 1995), 74–77.

8. *WJ*, June 11, 1881; Tetrault, *Myth of Seneca Falls*, 116.

9. Three additional volumes of *History of Woman Suffrage* were later published, with Ida Husted Harper as lead editor. Volume 4 was published in 1902; volumes 5 and 6 were published in 1922, long after the deaths of Anthony and Stanton.

10. Tetrault, *Myth of Seneca Falls*, 122.

11. *WJ*, June 11, 1881.

12. See, for example, Eleanor Flexner, *Century of Struggle* (Cambridge, MA: Harvard University Press, 1959, rev. 1996). Flexner, in turn, influenced many subsequent historians.

13. Flexner, *Century of Struggle*, 167–68.

14. *WJ*, May 13, 1871.

15. Hamand Venet, *A Strong Minded Woman: The Life of Mary A. Livermore* (Amherst: University of Massachusetts Press, 2005), 192.

16. Lois Bannister Merk, "Massachusetts and the Woman Suffrage Movement," (PhD diss., Radcliffe College, 1961), 373, n. 10.

17. *WJ*, June 20, 1874.

18. Ibid., January 24, 1874.

19. At the request of Stone, Campbell later wrote detailed descriptions of her work. *WJ*, July 21, 1894; July 28, 1894; August 4, 1894; August 11, 1894. This section relies on these articles.

20. *WJ*, January 1, 1876.

21. Kerr, *Lucy Stone*, 194.

22. *WJ*, December 25, 1886.

23. Ibid., December 31, 1881; April 1, 1882; May 2, 1885; June 23, 1888.

24. Alice Stone Blackwell Papers, Folder 19, WRC-SL.

Chapter 5

1. *WJ*, September 28, 1872; February 5, 1870.

2. Ibid., January 22, 1870.

3. Both admitted men also.

4. Rosalyn Terborg-Penn, *African American Women in the Struggle for the Vote, 1850–1920* (Indianapolis: Indiana University Press, 1998), 43–44.

5. Josephine Ruffin, *The Crisis*, August 1915.

6. McMillen, *Lucy Stone*, 176–77; Harriet Robinson, *Massachusetts in the Woman Suffrage Movement* (1883), 101–2.

7. *WJ*, March 30, 1872; Merk, "Massachusetts and the Woman Suffrage Movement," 43–44; NAWSA, *Woman Suffrage Yearbook 1917*, 32.

8. In 1870, the Irish Catholic population of Boston was nearly 35 percent. U.S. Bureau of the Census, "Historical Census Statistics on the Foreign-Born Population of the United States: 1850–1990."

9. *WJ*, January 31, 1874.

10. Ibid., September 16, 1876.

11. Merk, "Massachusetts and the Woman Suffrage Movement," 381; *WJ*, April 24, 1886.

12. WJ, July 30, 1881.

13. See generally Ruth Borden, *Woman and Temperance: The Quest for Power and Liberty, 1873–1900* (New Brunswick, NJ: Rutgers University Press).

14. *WJ*, January 30, 1875.

15. Ibid., May 31, 1879.

16. *Mass Moments*, "Concord Women Cast First Votes," March 29, 1880.

17. See, e.g., *WJ*, January 8, 1881; February 12, 1881.

18. *WJ*, March 25, 1882; Susan E. Marshall, *Splintered Sisterhood: Gender and Class in the Campaign against Woman Suffrage* (Madison: University of Wisconsin Press, 1997), 23-35.

19. Kate Gannett Wells, *An Argument Against Woman Suffrage*, 1885.

20. IV *HWS* 704; Woman Suffrage Yearbook 1917.

21. See generally Lois Bannister Merk, "Boston's Historic Public School Crisis," *New England Quarterly* (June 1958); Edmund B. Thomas Jr., "School Suffrage and the Campaign for Women's Suffrage in Massachusetts, 1879–1920," *Historical Journal of Massachusetts* (Winter 1997); Polly Welts Kaufman, *Boston Women and City School Politics, 1872–1905* (New York: Garland Publishing, 1994); *WJ*, December 24, 1888; January 5, 1889; October 6, 1888.

22. Thomas, "School Suffrage," 13; Kaufman, *Boston Women*, 155.

23. *Remonstrance*, 1891; Marshall, *Splintered Sisterhood*, 87.

24. *Stone v. Smith*, 159 Mass 413 (1893).

25. *WJ*, March 18, 1893.

26. Ibid., October 21, 1893.

27. Woman Suffrage Yearbook, 1917; *WJ*, December 23, 1893.

28. *Remonstrance*, 1894, 1895; IV *HWS* 734.

29. *WJ*, March 16, 1895; June 8, 1895; October 5, 1895; James J. Kenneally, "Woman Suffrage and the Massachusetts Referendum of 1895," *The Historian* (1968): 626.

30. *WJ*, October 5, 1895.

31. *Remonstrance*, 1896.

32. IV *HWS* 737–38.

33. Kenneally, "Woman Suffrage," 627.

34. *Remonstrance*, 1896.

35. *WJ*, November 9, 1895; November 16, 1895.

36. Maud Wood Park Papers, Pa-137, WRC-SL; Merk, "Massachusetts and the Woman Suffrage Movement," 330.

37. See, e.g., Kenneally, "Woman Suffrage," 632.

Chapter 6

1. All congressional vote data are from govtrack.us/congress.

2. *WJ*, April 9, 1887.

3. Ibid., Nov 26, 1887.

4. Jean Matthews, *The Rise of the New Woman, 1875–1930* (Chicago: Ivan R. Dee), 127.

5. Suzanne Marilley, *Woman Suffrage and the Origins of Liberal Feminism* (Cambridge, MA: Harvard University Press, 1996), 8.

6. Tetrault, *Myth of Seneca Falls*, 145.

7. Remarks of Lucy Stone, Report of the International Council of Women, Washington, D.C., March 25–April 1, 1888.

8. Tetrault, *Myth of Seneca Falls*, 153.

9. Ibid., 163.

10. John T. Cumbler, *From Abolition to Rights for All: The Making of a Reform Community in the Nineteenth Century* (Philadelphia: University of Pennsylvania Press, 2008), 116.

11. *WJ*, November 3, 1894.

12. Ibid., September 27, 1890.

13. Ibid., December 22, 1894.

14. Aileen S. Kraditor, *The Ideas of the Woman Suffrage Movement: 1890–1920* (New York: W.W. Norton, 1981), 131.

15. Proceedings of the Twenty-eighth Annual Convention of the National American Woman Suffrage Association, Washington, D.C., January 1896.

16. Sarah Graham, *Woman Suffrage and the New Democracy* (New Haven, CT: Yale University Press, 1996), 52.

17. Ibid., 7.

18. *WJ*, February 24, 1900.

19. See, e.g., Robert Booth Fowler, *Carrie Catt: Feminist Politician* (Boston: Northeastern University Press, 1986); Jacqueline Van Voris, *Carrie Chapman Catt: A Public Life* (New York: Feminist Press, 1987).

20. Woman Suffrage Calendar, 1900.

21. Graham, *Woman Suffrage*, 40, 47–48.

22. Johnson, Joan Marie. "Following the Money: Wealthy Women, Feminism, and the American Suffrage Movement," *Journal of Women's History* (2015): 62–87.

23. Graham, *Woman Suffrage*, 23; V *HWS* 59–60.

24. *WJ*, February 6, 1904.

25. Anna Howard Shaw, Eulogy for Susan B. Anthony, March 15, 1906; Valethia Watkins, "Votes for Women: Race, Gender, and W.E.B. Du Bois's Advocacy of Woman Suffrage," *Phylon* (Winter 2016): 3–19.

26. *The Crisis*, October 1911.

Chapter 7

1. New tactics are the subject of the next chapter.

2. Statistics in this section are from the United States Census Bureau; Jack Tager, and Richard W. Wilke, eds., *Historical Atlas of Massachusetts* (Amherst: University of Massachusetts, 1991), 34–39, 68, 82; Matthews, *Rise of the New Woman*, 11, 15, 49, 99; Rebecca Traister, *All the Single Ladies: Unmarried Women and the Rise of an Independent Nation* (New York: Simon & Schuster, 2016), 47; Carole Srole, "A Position that God Has Not Particularly Assigned to Men: The Feminization of Clerical Work, Boston, 1860–1915" (PhD diss., University of California–Los Angeles, 1984); Karen J. Blair, *The Clubwoman as Feminist: True Womanhood Redefined, 1868–1914* (New York: Holmes & Meier, 1980).

3. *New York World*, February 2, 1896.

4. Maud Wood Park Papers Pa-9, WRC-SL.

5. Maud Wood Park, "Who I Am and What I Believe," MWP Papers, LOC, collected in Melanie Gustafson, "Maud Wood Park Archive: The Power of Organization, Part One: Maud Wood Park and the Woman Suffrage Movement," part of Kathryn Kish Sklar and Thomas Dublin, eds.,

Women and Social Movements in the United States, 1600–2000 (hereafter, Park in Gustafson).

6. Maud Wood Park Papers, Pa-9, Folder 002690-047-001, WRC-SL.

7. Patricia Marzzacco, "The Obligation of Opportunity: Maud Wood Park, The College Equal Suffrage League, and the Response of Women Students in Massachusetts Colleges, 1900–1920" (PhD diss., Harvard University, 2004), 84–85.

8. She was known as Inez Haynes Gillmore after her first marriage. Following divorce and remarriage, she used the name Inez Haynes Irwin, though often published as Inez Haynes Gillmore.

9. *WJ*, April 25, 1914; Maud Wood Park Papers, Folders Pa-9, Pa-175, Pa-137, 002690-047-0001, WRC-SL; Mary Hutcheson Page Papers, Folder 653-653b, WRC-SL.

10. Maud Wood Park Papers, Folders Pa-9, Pa-175, Pa-137, 002690-047-0001, WRC-SL.

11. Maud Wood Park Papers, Folder 002690-047-0001, WRC-SL.

12. *WJ*, March 31, 1900.

13. Marzzacco, "Obligation of Opportunity," 30.

14. Maud Wood Park Papers, Folder 137, WRC-SL.

15. Ibid.

16. V *HWS* 171, 192–93.

17. Maud Wood Park, "An explanation as to why Bob and I were not publicly married is probably needed," Park in Gustafson, Document 3. Park also explained that her plan for her round-the-world trip had been made before she decided to remarry.

18. Maud Wood Park Papers, Folder Pa-175, WRC-SL.

19. James Kenneally, *Women and American Trade Unions* (Montreal: Eden Press, 1981), 18. The percentage of male industrialized workers who were unionized was similar, but the absolute number was far higher because of their greater participation in the workforce. The percentage of the male labor force composed of union members would grow tremendously during the next several decades.

20. Thomas Juravich, et al. *Commonwealth of Toil: Chapters in the History of Massachusetts Workers and Their Unions* (Amherst: University of Massachusetts, 1996), 87–89.

21. V *HWS* 189–91.

22. Kenneally, *Women and American Trade*, 131; Alexander Keyssar, *The Right to Vote: The Contested History of Democracy in the United States* (New York: Basic Books, 2000), 164.

23. Mary Kenney, O'Sullivan, *Why the Working Woman Needs the Vote*.

24. Kenneally, *Women and American Trade*, 54; Sharon Hartman Strom, *Political Woman: Florence Luscomb and the Legacy of Radical Reform* (Philadelphia: Temple University Press, 2001), 70.

25. Teresa Blue Holden, "Earnest Women Can Do Anything: The Public Career of Josephine St. Pierre Ruffin 1842–1904" (PhD diss., St. Louis University, 2005).

26. *Woman's Era*, March 1894.

27. Ibid., March, June, July, November 1894.

28. Ibid., August 1895.

29. Graham, *Woman Suffrage*, 23–25. There were some exceptions during state campaigns, however. NAWSA's policy might be described as courting white southerners but courting black northerners during individual state campaigns. See Terborg-Penn, *African American Women*, 92–105, 126.

30. *WJ*, February 9, 1901; June 16, 1900.

Chapter 8

1. Sharon Hartman Strom, "Leadership and Tactics in the American Woman Suffrage Movement: A New Perspective from Massachusetts," *Journal of American History* 62 (September 1975): 300.

2. See, e.g., Holly McCammon, "Out of the Parlors and into the Streets: The Changing Tactical Repertoire of the U.S. Women's Suffrage Movements," *Social Forces* (March 2003): 787.

3. Maud Wood Park Papers, Folder 94, WRC-SL.

4. Ibid., Folder 95, WRC-SL.

5. Emmeline Pankhurst, *My Own Story* (1914), 129. The English movement would later engage in a campaign that included window breaking and other forms of property damage.

6. Ellen Carol DeBois, *Woman Suffrage & Women's Rights* (New York: NYU Press, 1998), 195–99.

7. *WJ*, September 19, 1908.

8. Florence Luscomb Papers, Folder 635. WRC-SL.

9. Ibid.; V *HWS* 276.

10. Florence Luscomb Papers, Folder 635, MC 394: Folder 212, WRC-SL.

11. Teresa O'Leary Crowley Papers, Folder 49, WRC-SL.

12. Jennie Loitman Barron, *Jewish Women's Archive*; https://www.radcliffe.harvard.edu/schlesinger-library/blog/freedom-all.

13. Margaret Foley Papers, Folder 3, WRC-SL.

14. Maud Wood Park Papers, Folder 95, WRC-SL.

15. Florence Luscomb Papers, Folder 635, WRC-SL; *WJ*, August 28, 1909.

16. *WJ*, August 28, 1909.

17. Margaret Foley Papers, MC 404: Folder 55, WRC-SL.

18. *WJ*, August 28, 1909.

19. Ibid., October 30, 1909.

20. Ibid.

21. Graham, *Woman Suffrage*, 54.

22. *WJ*, April 30, 1910.

23. Maud Wood Park Papers, Folder 95, WRC-SL.

24. Historian Susan Ware, conversation with the author.

25. Virginia Scharff, *Taking the Wheel: Women and the Coming of the Motor Age* (New York: The Free Press, 1991), 79.

26. *WJ*, November 12, 1910; Margaret Foley Papers, Folder 72, WRC-SL; Florence Luscomb Papers, MC 394: Folder 12, WRC-SL.

27. Maud Wood Park Papers, Folder 95, WRC-SL.

28. Ibid.

29. *Globe*, May 17, 1910.

30. *Globe*, March 12, 1911.

31. Maud Wood Park Papers, Folder 21, WRC-SL.

32. *Globe*, October 1, 1911; *WJ*, November 12, 1910; Florence Luscomb Papers, 394: Folder 212, WRC-SL.

33. *WJ*, February 26, 1910; December 23, 1911; March 30, 1912; October 5, 1912.

34. *Muller v. Oregon*, 208 U.S. 412 (1908); Louis Brandeis, Speech on Suffrage at Tremont Temple, October 12, 1915.

35. *WJ*, October 14, 1911; *Globe*, October 13, 1911; October 17; 1911.

36. Pankhurst, *My Own Story*, 171; *Harvard Crimson*, December 2, 1911; December 7, 1911; *WJ*, December 9, 1911.

37. Johnson, *Following the Money*, 67.

38. Florence Luscomb Papers, Folder 635, MC: 394, Folder 212, WRC-SL.

39. *Globe*, October 15, 1911.

40. Foss was not a typical Democrat. He was a former Republican who broke with the party over tariffs.

Chapter 9

1. *NYT*, August 31, 1912.
2. V *HWS* 708.
3. Inez Hayes Irwin, *The Story of the Woman's Party* (1921), 4.
4. Adapted from Laurel Thatcher Ulrich's comment that well-behaved women seldom make history.
5. *WJ*, March 8, 1913.
6. Remembering the Woman Suffrage Parade of 1913, LOC.
7. *Suffragist*, December 6, 1913.
8. *WJ*, June 19, 1915.
9. Flexner, *Century of Struggle*, 262, 376.
10. V *HWS* 315.
11. *Globe*, January 29, 1913.
12. Margaret Foley Papers, Folder 72, WRC-SL.

Chapter 10

1. Florence Luscomb Papers, MC 393: Folder 212, WRC-SL.
2. Woman Suffrage Yearbook 1917.
3. Due to differences of opinion that developed in the last year of the campaign, Park withdrew from the Big Four and concentrated her efforts on Suffolk County. Park, Folder 94, WRC-SL.
4. Mary Hutcheson Page Papers, Folder 23, WRC-SL.
5. Maud Wood Park Papers, Folder 148, WRC-SL; *Globe*, May 3, 1914.
6. Maud Wood Park Papers, Folder 148, WRC-SL; *Globe*, May 3, 1914; Luscomb, MC 394: Folder 212, WRC-SL.
7. VI *HWS* 284.
8. Graham, *Woman Suffrage*, 63, 67.
9. *Globe*, June 26, 1915; VI *HWS* 286l Florence Seaver Slocomb Papers, Box 1, Folder 13, SSC-SC.
10. Susan Ware, *Partner and I: Molly Dewson, Feminism, and New Deal Politics* (New Haven, CT: Yale University Press, 1989), 68.
11. Florence Luscomb Papers, Folder 635, WRC-SL; *Globe*, October 25, 1915.
12. *Globe*, October 10, 1915; October 21, 1915; *Worcester Evening Post*, October 23, 1915; VI *HWS* 285.

13. Racism was very much on the minds of Boston's blacks in 1915. When D.W. Griffith's film *Birth of a Nation* opened in Boston in April, the city's black community protested against the film.

14. *The Crisis*, August 1915.

15. Melissa R. Klapper, *Ballots, Babies, Banners of Peace: American Jewish Women's Activism, 1890–1940* (New York: NYU Press, 2013), 33–34.

16. Ibid., 28.

17. Catholic for Suffrage leaflets, Suffrage Collection, Box 2, Folder 1, SSC-SC.

18. *Globe*, July 8, 1915; July 11, 1915; August 11, 1915; Foley Folder 63, WRC-SL.

19. *Globe*, September 18, 1915; October 27, 1915; October 29, 1915; October 31, 1915.

20. Ibid., October 3, 1915; October 23, 1915; October 24, 1915; *Worcester Evening Post*, October 30, 1915.

21. Flier, Torchlight Suffrage March and Mass Meeting, Worcester, Massachusetts, Ann Lewis Women's Suffrage Collection, http:// lewissuffragecollection.omeka.net/items/show/1468.

22. *NYT*, February 6, 1915.

23. *Remonstrance*, October 1915; *Boston Journal*, October 30, 1915; Florence Seaver Slocomb Papers, Box 1, Folder 1, SSC-SC.

24. *Globe*, September 24, 1915.

25. *Globe*, October 20, 1915.

26. Park Folder 94, WRC-SL; VI *HWS* 287–88.

27. *WJ*, November 6, 1915.

28. Park, Folder 94, WRC-SL.

29. *WJ*, November 13, 1915.

Chapter 11

1. See, e.g., Nancy F. Cott, "Historical Perspectives: The Equal Rights Amendment Conflict in the 1920s," in *Conflicts in Feminism*, edited by Marianne Hirsch and Evelyn Fox Keller (New York: Routledge, 1990), 44-59.

2. Johnson, *Following the Money*, 76–79.

3. Christine Stansell uses the mother-daughter analogy in *The Feminist Promise: 1792 to the Present* (New York: Random House, 2010).

4. V *HWS* 460–61.

5. Ibid.

6. Flexner, *Century of Struggle*, 267.

7. J.D. Zahniser, and Amelia R. Fry, *Alice Paul: Claiming Power* (Oxford: Oxford University Press, 2014), 234.

8. Ibid., 218; see "National Suffrage and the Race Problem," *Suffragist*, November 14, 1914.

9. *NYT*, September 9, 1916.

10. Carrie Chapman Catt and Nettie Rogers Shuler, *Woman Suffrage and Politics: The Inner Story of the Suffrage Movement* (New York: Charles Scribner's Sons, 1926), 262–63. There is no surviving list of the states that endorsed the Winning Plan.

11. Maud Wood Park, *Front Door Lobby* (Boston: Beacon Press, 1960), 17.

12. Ibid., 25.

13. Catt and Shuler, *Woman Suffrage*, 266–67; V *HWS* 171.

14. *WJ*, June 2, 1917.

15. Park, *Front Door Lobby*, 23.

16. V HWS 723.

17. *WJ*, November 17, 1917.

18. *WJ*, June 2, 1917; November 10, 1917; November 17, 1917.

19. Ibid., June 30, 1917.

20. See, e.g., Susan Goodier, and Karen Postorello, *Women Will Vote: Winning Suffrage in New York State.* (Ithaca, NY: Cornell University Press, 2017).

21. Michigan, North Dakota, Nebraska, and Indiana were the others—Ohio did as well, but the grant was quickly revoked.

22. *WJ*, November 10, 1917; V *HWS* 525.

23. *WJ*, January 19, 1918.

24. Park, *Front Door Lobby*, 157.

25. Maud Wood Park to Robert Freeman Hunter, March 24, 1918, and April 26, 1918, Park in Gustafson, Documents 35 and 36.

26. *WJ*, October 5, 1918.

27. Ibid., October 19, 1918.

28. VI *HWS* 300; Grace Allen Johnson Papers, MC 193, Folder 175, WRC-SL.

29. Teresa Crowley Papers, Folder 49. Luscomb MC 394: Folder 212, WRC-SL.

30. *WJ*, November 9, 1918.

31. Park, *Front Door Lobby*, 233.

32. *Globe*, February 25, 1919. See generally Anita C. Danker, "Grassroots Suffragists: Josephine Collins and Louise Mayo, A Study in Contrasts," *New England Journal of History* (Spring 2011): 54–72.

33. *Globe*, February 25, 1919; February 27, 1919.

34. Ibid., February 24, 1919; March 11, 1919.

35. Florence Luscomb Papers, MC 394: Folder 212, WRC-SL.

36. *Globe*, June 13, 1919; Margaret Foley, MC 404: Folder 73, WRC-SL.

37. *Globe*, June 13, 1919; *WJ*, July 5, 1919.

38. *WJ*, August 28, 1920; September 23, 1920; *NYT*, August 27, 1920.

39. *WJ*, September 6, 1919; *Globe*, September 23, 1920; Florence Luscomb Papers, MC 393: Folder 212, WRC-SL.

INDEX

ABOUT THE AUTHOR

Barbara F. Berenson is the author of *Boston and the Civil War: Hub of the Second Revolution* (The History Press, 2014) and *Walking Tours of Civil War Boston: Hub of Abolitionism* (The Freedom Trail Foundation, 2011, 2nd ed. 2014). She is the coeditor of *Breaking Barriers: The Unfinished Story of Women Lawyers and Judges in Massachusetts* (Massachusetts Continuing Legal Education, 2012). A graduate of Harvard College and Harvard Law School, she works as a senior attorney at the Massachusetts Supreme Judicial Court. Please visit www.barbarafberenson.com.